To the Ends of the Earth:

Building a
National Missionary
Sending Structure

Arto Hämäläinen and Ulf Strohbehn

WIPF & STOCK · Eugene, Oregon

Wipf and Stock Publishers
199 W 8th Ave, Suite 3
Eugene, OR 97401

To the Ends of the Earth
Building a National Missionary Sending Structure
By Hamalainen, Arto and Strohbehn, Ulf
Copyright © 2020 APTS Press All rights reserved.
Softcover ISBN-13: 978-1-7252-6992-7
Hardcover ISBN-13: 978-1-7252-6994-1
eBook ISBN-13: 978-1-7252-6993-4
Publication date 2/20/2020
Previously published by APTS, 2020

This edition is a scanned facsimile of the original edition published in 2020.

Table of Contents

In *To the Ends of the Earth: Building a National Missionary Sending Structure*, Dr. Arto Hämäläinen and Dr. Ulf Strohbehn provide a framework for building a national mission structure, based on many years of effective high-level leadership on the platform of a Spirit-filled collaborative community worldwide. Arto has been a good friend of more than three decades whom I have observed providing insightful anointed leadership in the cause of God's mission in this world. Ulf Strohbehn contributes insightful perspective as a cultural anthropologist serving for fifteen years in Malawi.

The authors emphasize the need for Spirit-empowered key people, who are properly purposed to design an effective national mission structure built and operated with wise decision making from a biblical and practical perspective frame, with clarity and conviction. Their reflections represent an emerging Spirit-filled coalescing, collaborative, community described in *Together in One Mission: Pentecostal Cooperation in World Evangelization*, which poses great potential for a macro impulse in God's agenda in and through building national mission structures for such a time as this.

Dr. Luis Bush
International Facilitator
Transform World Connections
Servant Catalyst
4/14 Movement
Chancellor
Cornerstone International University (CIU)
Servant
Transform World 2020

Hämäläinen and Strohbehn have written an excellent book that many have been waiting for. *To the Ends of the Earth: Building a National Missionary Sending Structure* will prove to be especially beneficial to the younger, dramatically growing churches in the non-Western world and instructive to all who have a heart and mind for what the Lord of the Harvest is doing in our broken world.

Dr. Peter Kuzmic
Paul E. and Eva B. Toms Distinguished Professor of World Missions and European Studies
Gordon-Conwell Theological Seminary

In 1792 William Carey published his famous treatise known as *An Enquiry into the Obligations of Christians to Use Means for the Conversion of the Heathen.* To "use means" meant, of course, the creation of the first Protestant missionary structure which sparked the modern missionary movement. Since that time thousands of mission organizations have arisen, all with the goal to bring the Gospel to the ends of the earth. Yet, these organizations operate mostly independently of one another and collaboration is more the exception than the rule. Arto Hämäläinen and Ulf Strohbehn in *To the Ends of the Earth: Building a National Mission Structure* provide a roadmap for greater global collaboration in fulfilling the Great Commission. They show the practical dynamics of missions' strategy and structure, but all within the larger context of the Spirit's dynamic work in and through the Church.

Dr. Timothy C. Tennent
President
Asbury Theological Seminary
Professor of World Christianity
Asbury Theological Seminary

As mission becomes more and more pluricentric and new initiatives emerge around the globe, particularly in the Global South, this book is a helpful tool and an invaluable gift to the worldwide mission community.

To the Ends of the Earth: Building a National Missionary Sending Structure, written by my dear friend Dr. Arto Hämäläinen and his colleague Dr. Ulf Strohbehn, is an excellent guide for the establishment of a sending and supporting mission structure. This book is not just for those who are starting a national mission movement, but also for the already existing movements that need to evaluate their priorities and the current relevance of their structures. The combination of biblical principles and of good practical examples makes the material easy to follow and to apply in any context. I fully recommend this book as a good example of a reflective practitioner approach to such an important aspect of providing excellence and effectiveness in missionary work.

Rev. Dr. Bertil Ekström
Associated Director
World Evangelical Alliance (WEA) Mission Commission

To the Ends of the Earth: Building a National Missionary Sending Structure, a remarkable manual on building and sustaining national mission structures is an amazingly useful and insightful blend of time-tested practical experience, biblical teaching, organizational and leadership theory applied to grassroots problems, and seasoned, careful reflection. No other Pentecostal missiologist has such a massive and diverse experience concerning national mission structures than Dr. Arto Hämäläinen. Collaboration with his younger missiologist-theologian colleague has resulted in a unique resource for all interested in spreading the Gospel of Christ to every people. Highly recommended.

Rev. Dr. Veli-Matti Kärkkäinen
Professor of Systematic Theology
Fuller Theological Seminary
Docent of Theology, Faculty of Theology
University of Helsinki

Two practitioner-scholars of Pentecostal mission have produced an extremely useful tool for Spirit-filled communities to organize themselves to fuel the sustained growth of global Christianity into the future. *To the Ends of the Earth: Building a National Missionary Sending Structure* is timely for Spirit-empowered mission to have practical components, while positioning mission communities towards decentralized local operations closely engaging given contexts.

Dr. Wonsuk Ma
Dean
College of Theology and Ministry, Distinguished Professor of
Global Christianity
Oral Roberts University

For every successful entity knowledge is very important. "You cannot do a do unless you know how to do." It saves time and costs if the knowledge is given by an experienced practical person. Dr. Arto and Dr Ulf have both knowledge and skill about reaching the unreached. With the vast global experience in leadership and Bible teachings, I find *To the Ends of the Earth: Building a National Missionary Sending Structure* a blend of sound doctrine, ethical and practical Missionary handbook. It is an eye opener and guide to those who seek workable solutions in the modern world to reach the unreached with The Gospel of our Lord. It will be a helpful tool in the hands of your missionary organization.

Bishop Eli Rop
General Secretary
Full Gospel Churches of Kenya
Secretary
Africa Pentecostal Mission Fellowship (APMF)

For many years, churches and mission practitioners in Africa have been struggling to obey the Great Commission, through their own culture and experience, by sending out missionaries without proper guiding tool or sustainable structure. I congratulate the authors of *To the Ends of the Earth: Building a National Missionary Sending Structure* on their achievement, as they have used their professions and matured practical experience in missions to write this valuable book. This book will be used by many as a readily available resource to pursue the best practices in world missions.

I conclude by expressing my deepest appreciation to Dr. Arto Hämäläinen and Dr. Ulf Strohbehn for this wonderful contribution towards reaching the unreached.

Rev. Benjamin W. Rutashoborwa
Mission Director
The Free Pentecostal Churches of Tanzania

The knowledge and experience of Dr. Arto Hämäläinen and Dr. Ulf Strohbehn in missions have influenced thousands of students on many different continents during decades of service. They have not only inspired and trained missionary candidates, which have been used to receive support from abroad, they have also developed successful strategies and structures for new sending movements and churches.

Hämäläinen and Strohbehn have a special heart for unreached people groups, and they understand the importance of releasing the hidden resources from new sending countries. They explain how resources can be released by mentoring and training. Hämäläinen and Strohbehn have increased interest among churches in Europe, Africa, Asia and South America to finish the Great Commission of Jesus Christ.

It is a great pleasure and blessing to get their best portion of teaching in written form, where a sound balance between theology and practice are easily seen. I think *To the Ends of the Earth: Building a National Missionary Sending Structure* will change the future of a new missionary generation, when the whole Church will be able to preach the full gospel to all the nations.

Rauli Lehtonen
Mission pastor
Filadelfia Stockholm

The book, *To the Ends of the Earth: Building a National Missionary Sending Structure*, presents a blend of theology, missiology and practical guidelines for missions. This book reminds us that the Church has no alternative to missions, and missions is impossible without the Holy Spirit. Therefore, the call of this book is that church leaders should be Holy Spirit-driven mission builders. This is how evangelism needs can be met and spiritual mandates fulfilled.

Joseph Dimitrov, PhD
President
Continental Theological Seminary

Missionary work without a clear strategy and structure often results in repeating past mistakes. *To the Ends of the Earth: Building a National Missionary Sending Structure* sheds light into the significance of these supporting elements. Without a healthy and mutual equilibrium, strategy and structure alone will not suffice. The writers of this book give us a clear reminder of the role that the Holy Spirit plays in the formation of these supporting structures. Through defining the role of the Holy Spirit, the overall "Why" of missionary work becomes evident. This creates a foundation for developing a clear "How" and "What" for strategic direction and operational structure.

Dr. Ari Joensuu
Regional Director
Africa, Central Asia, Latin America, and Middle East/Fida International

Throughout the history of the world Christian movement, effective and lasting missional expansion has been marked by the Biblical balance of spontaneity and structure. In an exciting new time of emerging missionary sending movements around the world, this excellent book, *To the Ends of the Earth: Building a National Missionary Sending Structure*, provides a literary platform for cooperation and collaboration in world mission. This is the way forward for the global Great Commission community.

Dr. Grant McClung
President
Missions Resource Group
Missiological Advisor
World Missions Commission of the Pentecostal World Fellowship

To the Ends of the Earth: Building a National Missionary Sending Structure is certainly a precious tool for renewing the vision for missions at all levels, whether in the local church or in para-ecclesiastic organizations. It is a practical manual that will help educate believers in the fulfillment of the most important, yet often neglected objective of the church: missions!

Special thanks to its authors for providing a solid biblical theology for missions, and effective keys to implement God's mission in our generation. A truly captivating, inspiring read awaits you. May it renew our resolve to help others respond to God's Call: "Here I am, send me!"

Rev. Daniel Costanza
Senior Pastor
Brussels Christian Center
Executive Director
Pentecostal European Fellowship (PEF)

To the Ends of the Earth: Building a National Missionary Sending Structure is strategically important to new missionary sending nations and agencies in Asia and Africa. It provides valuable insight and wisdom from the many years of experience of the missionary statesman, Dr. Arto Hämäläinen. At a time when God is raising up new nations to take the Gospel to the "ends of the Earth," it is vital to develop the right structure to sustain and energize such missions' endeavors. I recommend this book to every national leader to inspire and guide your nation's journey to the "ends of the Earth."

Rev. Michael Dissanayeke
General Superintendent
Assemblies of God Sri Lanka
Member, Lead
Team of the Mission Commission of the World Assemblies of God
Fellowship
Member World Missions Commission of Pentecostal World Fellowship

Doctors Arto Hämäläinen and Ulf Strohbehn have created an amazing mission manual for the use of churches and leaders in *To the Ends of the Earth: Building a National Missionary Sending Structure.* I have had the privilege to closely follow Arto`s path to one of leading Pentecostal mission promoters in Europe and in all the world over two decades. He has a God-given gift to share biblical treasures and principles of mission structures understandably for today's reader. Arto Hämäläinen and Ulf Strohbehn humbly and practically knit together a deep understanding of the need of flexibility in various sending situations with the leading authority of the Holy Spirit. As a former conductor of a symphony orchestra, Arto has a unique ability to dig out the best talents of national resources and benefits for the fulfillment of Jesus`s Great Commission.

Rev. Rauno Mikkonen
Chairman
Pentecostal European Mission Committee

Dr. Arto Hämäläinen is a long-term friend. I appreciate his thinking in various capacities. While the "Missional Scenario is changing globally," I recommend *To the Ends of the Earth: Building a National Missionary Sending Structure.* Dr. Arto has walked the talk for so long. He is a seasoned missional thinker with a lot of experience. He relates the global scenario very well. Both Arto Hämäläinen and Ulf Strohbehn have done well in their book. They have provoked us to think. However, in the contemporary world, missional activities are changing, and evangelistic challenges are also changing, but the Gospel is the same. I echo the apostle Paul's sentiment of Rom 1:16, "For I am not ashamed of the gospel: for it is the power of God unto salvation to everyone that believeth; to the Jew first, and also to the Greek" (ASV).

Dr. K. Rajendran
Chairman
Global Innovative Voices & Associates (GIVA Trust), Giva-Inno-Ventures Pvt. Ltd.

Being involved in the Great Commission is not an option, but an obligation for every believer and every church. When a national church understands its responsibility to be part of the Great Commission, creating a functional sending structure is a fundamental element in achieving this goal. Dr. Arto Hämäläinen's and Dr. Ulf Strohbehn's book, *To the Ends of the Earth: Building a National Missionary Sending Structure,* is like a recipe that presents all those ingredients that are essential to start and successfully maintain such a structure. The Romanian Pentecostal Foreign Mission Agency has benefited greatly from Dr. Hämäläinen's expertise in becoming one of the youngest and most dynamic Pentecostal mission agencies. That is why I strongly recommend this book, especially to mission leaders, whether they are just starting to create a sending structure, or they are running an agency with a history in world missions that needs reinventing from time to time.

Rev Gheorghe Ritisan
President
APME (Romanian Pentecostal Foreign Mission Agency)
Vice-chairman of Pentecostal European Mission (PEM)

I've known Arto Hämäläinen for many years. It has been a pleasure to work with him on the Pentecostal World Fellowship Missions Commission. I appreciate his heart to see the "receivers become new senders." I've seen that be a part of his focus and leadership in different networks he has led and chaired.

He has authored *To the Ends of the Earth: Building a National Missionary Sending Structure which* is a relevant and practical tool to help the new senders engage many of the practical issues that confront them. This book is a welcome resource for us to move forward, and take the vision and involvement of national movements starting out in missions to the next level.

Brad Walz
Chairman
World Assemblies of God Fellowship (WAGF) Missions' Commission

To the Ends of the Earth: Building a National Missionary Sending Structure is authored by Dr. Arto Hämäläinen with Dr. Ulf Strohbehn. This book serves strategic directions for those who are new to missions sending.

Dr. Arto is the champion for the cause of missions in newly sending countries. He is passionate about seeing a great missionary movement in the nations which have been on the receiving end of missionaries. This book is very practical and has different perspectives in writing, taking into consideration the limitations and challenges each mission faces. I am sure this book will be great manual and guide for those who wish to begin a new missions' structure for sending missionaries. Let the blessings of Pentecostal missions flow!

Rev. Asa M. Kain
Chairman
Pentecostal Asia Mission (PAM)
Vice Chair
World Missions Commission of the Pentecostal World Fellowship

The two significant parts of *To the Ends of the Earth: Building a National Missionary Sending Structure* each make a specific contribution. The brief overview of a uniquely Pentecostal theology of mission is very worthwhile. The latter part of the book aims to put an experienced head on the shoulders of younger churches, movements and denominations moving into missions in an active way. It contains so much that it will be well worth reading a second time to get the best out of it.

Rev Dr Kevin Hovey (ML)
Senior Lecturer and Head of Department, Pastoral and Cross-Cultural Ministry
Alphacruxis College, Australia

Foreword

There are few people who have had a more consistent leadership role in Christian world missions than Arto Hämäläinen. Now he has teamed up with Ulf Strohbehn to make yet another meaningful contribution to the global cause of Christ.

Building a National Mission Structure is written as a manual but this should not distract from its inspirational and motivational value. As seasoned advisors and consultants, the authors bring vast experience to the subject of how to facilitate missionary enterprise by building an effective supportive structure. Their depth of experience is evident in that this book is not simply a "how to" list of procedures but is missiological motivation enabling mission leaders to clearly establish the "why" of missionary endeavor.

Particularly noticeable and commendable, this book successfully translates the well-established models of Western missionary structures into virtually any national church context. As global mission increasingly enjoys greater resourcing and personnel in the developing world this emphasis is most important. Masterfully, Hämäläinen and *Strohbehn* have written a book that should be a valuable tool in the hands of any missionary-minded leader anywhere in the world.

This book is unapologetically Pentecostal in its orientation and theology. This should not be a surprise knowing the authors but the theology presented in this book is so biblically sound that the contents will have great value to all, regardless of denominational background. The consistent return to the work of the Holy Spirit throughout this book is one of its most commendable features.

As an educator, it would be my hope that this book is widely adopted as a text in Bible Colleges and Seminaries around the world.

It certainly adds to the volumes currently available to educators but is so succinct in covering the subject that it should be a very useful text for classroom instruction. At the very least it should find its way on reading lists and recommended sources for those engaged in missiological study at any level.

I heartily recommend this very useful and well-written volume.

Paul R Alexander, PhD
Chair, World Alliance for Pentecostal Theological Education
President, Trinity Bible College and Graduate School, Ellendale, North Dakota, USA

Preface

During the last number of decades, I have observed the development of world mission sending agencies in many countries. I have watched this process while serving as Executive Director of Fida International (the Finnish Pentecostal Mission organization), as chairman of the World Missions Commission of the Pentecostal World Fellowship (PWF) and of the Pentecostal European Fellowship (PEF) and also its mission branch, the Pentecostal European Mission (PEM), as advisor of the Pentecostal Asia Mission (PAM), and recently as chairman of the African Pentecostal Mission Consultation (APMC). I have been privileged also to see the growth of mission endeavours of the World Assemblies of God Fellowship (WAGF) as a member of the leadership team of its Mission Commission. An even larger picture has opened to me through connections in the Lausanne Movement and the World Evangelical Alliance (WEA). I have personally been involved in mission training in about 60 countries.

The birth of many new mission organizations and mission departments tells me that God is interested in seeing the Great Commission fulfilled and every people group to be reached as soon as possible. At the same time, the need to create fruitful and sustainable structures for world missions is increasing. Therefore I have been eager to provide a tool for such development in cooperation with the Bible and mission education coach and advisor of Fida International, Dr. Ulf Strohbehn, who also serves the wider Pentecostal family in training challenges.

This book does not attempt to give answers to every question concerning mission structures. It is written to give a basic road map for the organizing of a mission agency, but every denomination and mission organization must determine the best structure for its own context. Without a map we may be lost, but with a map, one will find different paths, sometimes longer but more beautiful, sometimes quicker and smoother. Although this book is authored by writers from the West, we have tried to look at the world from a multicultural perspective.

This is a map, a tool, and a vehicle by which to pursue the best practices in world missions. Closely related to this theme, I have also written a book entitled *How to Start Missionary Work in New Sending Countries* (Fida International, 2003, revised edition2014). I recommend studying that book as well. In this present book, the focus is concentrated on building the structure of the mission agency.

I trust this book will provide assistance to those who are seriously desiring help in designing a structure for a world missions sending agency.

Arto Hämäläinen
Vantaa, Finland January 3, 2019

Introduction

For the New Testament church, missions were its reason for existence. The birth of the church in Jerusalem was the fulfillment of Jesus' promise of the outpouring of the Holy Spirit. Connected to that promise was his pronouncement of the missionary task: "You will be my witnesses in Jerusalem, and in all Judea, Samaria and to the ends of the earth" (Acts 1:8). The church's influence was not only felt in Jerusalem but reached even to Ethiopia and to Antioch, which then became the base for the spreading of the Gospel to the Gentiles through the ministry of the apostle Paul and his co-workers (Acts 8 and 11).

We can notice quite clearly how the churches that Paul and his team established became missions-minded and sent out missionaries. We see a glimpse of that in Acts 20:4: "He was accompanied by Sopater son of Pyrrhus from Berea, Aristarchus and Secundus from Thessalonica, Gaius from Derbe, Timothy also, and Tychicus and Trophimus from the province of Asia." Here, the churches in Berea, Thessalonica, Derbe, and Lystra (Timothy's home church) are mentioned. Paul was instrumental in establishing the churches in Ephesus and in all of Asia Minor. His Bible, or mission, school in Ephesus was very effective, causing the spread of the Gospel to the whole province of Asia (Acts 19:10). He himself did not go everywhere but, through his training ministry, multiplied churches and manpower for spreading the Gospel.

The New Testament also shows us that the church in Philippi sent Epaphroditus, whom Paul called "a co-

---

[1] All Scripture quoted in this book are from the New International Version (NIV).

worker and fellow soldier" (Phil. 2:25). He used the term "your messenger" to describe the relationship of Epaphroditus to the Philippians. "Messenger" is translated from the Greek word *apostolon*, which means one who has been sent (and in a special context, "apostle"), and is actually the root for the English word "missionary" via the Latin word *missio*, which also includes the meaning of "sending."

From the time of Paul, women have played a significant role in missions history. Phoebe was one of his co-workers; while serving as a deacon in Cenchreae, she also served in bringing his letter to the church in Rome (Rom. 16:1-2). In that letter, he instructed the Romans to receive her "in a way worthy of his people." We learn also that she had been a benefactor to others as well as Paul, thus his admonition that she be cared for in a practical way while in Rome. Paul was not like some enthusiastic people of today who just send missionaries to a foreign country without thinking of what their needs may be in that country or of its cultural context. Paul focused on sustainable results, which necessitated a proper sending structure.

Phoebe was not the only female co-worker with Paul. In many of the greetings in his letters we find long lists of women who contributed greatly to the expansion of God's Kingdom. For instance, in Roman 13:3, he speaks of Priscilla (after again mentioning Phoebe). We know that in Corinth, Priscilla worked with her husband Aquila, along with Paul, and they all had the same secular job as tentmakers. As a couple, Aquila and Priscilla also became a great blessing to the church in Ephesus. Couples, families, and also singles are all needed in cultivating a healthy church.

Later in history, the missional character of the Church weakened and almost faded away as the Church tended to turn inward, losing the nature of the early church. Missions became a matter for those in monasteries who were especially interested in it. Unfortunately, the Reformation did not bring about any major change in this respect. And because the role of monasteries disappeared in the Protestant context, mission vision was fatally weakened. Although the Anabaptists made some significant attempts to revive missions, a greater growth in missions came through the Protestant mission societies. However, even at that time, the Protestant churches did not take that role of missions as a fulfillment of the Great Commission, so they had no structure for missions. Thus, mission agencies, that were started because of the vision of some missions-minded individuals, took over the missionary work.

Beginning around 1800, through the influence of William Carey and others, churches started to establish their own mission societies (i.e., Baptist mission, Lutheran mission). When the Pentecostal revival touched the world at the beginning of the 20th century, this new movement was highly missions oriented. From Azusa Street, the revival spread quickly to other continents, for the Holy Spirit is the missionary Spirit. However, because Pentecostal churches were often influenced by various other traditions, their world missions structures were diverse. One of the main reasons for the formation of the Assemblies of God (AG) USA in 1914 was to provide a legal structure for world missions. Its practical solution was to form a missions department in its national structure. That model has been followed by AG churches all over the world. Because some of the World Assemblies of God Fellowship member churches were not established by AG missionaries, their structures are different from the USA AG structure.

Some Pentecostal churches have a singular centralized authority extending globally (e.g., Foursquare, Church of God/Tennessee, Church of God in Christ, International Pentecostal Holiness Church), which influences their missions structures as well. In the Nordic countries of Europe, there is a strong emphasis on the role of the local church, which has influenced their world mission work. However, some national coordinating mission structures have become necessary in those Nordic countries also. The central question then has been, "What is the role of the local church and the national missions department or organization?"

Structures in the Pentecostal context have not been limited to the national level. Continental and global networks have been built which hold unity and cooperation as important values. This approach can be either pragmatic or more theologically based, but it always emphasizes the unity and cooperation of the churches in the body of Christ.

Because of the tremendous growth of Pentecostal-Charismatic churches over the last decades, new challenges have appeared. The "Global South" has become the centre of gravity for evangelical and

Pentecostal churches. At the same time, these new growing churches have awakened to the challenge of the Great Commission and are now the primary resource of power for the completion of the missions task. But how should they build their mission structures? What can we learn from the teachings of the Bible? What can we learn from mission history? The aim of this book is to reflect on the Great commission and offer tools for building a strong mission structure.

Chapter 1

What is Needed to Start a Missions Program

Three elements are essential for an effective missions program: Holy Spirit-empowered people, a missions strategy, and the structure to implement that strategy. Jesus promised to provide his disciples with power to preach the Gospel, from Jerusalem to the ends of the earth (Acts 1:8). They were not able to implement that task in their own power, or by trusting just in their former experiences. Second, they needed a strategy. Third, a structure was necessary in order to ensure the desired results. The local churches' cooperation formed a firm foundation for fulfilling the Great Commission. Pentecost was the birthday of the Church. We will look at each of the three elements below.

Holy Spirit-Empowered People

The outpouring of the Holy Spirit in Jerusalem enabled the people to become witnesses for Jesus Christ, for the Holy Spirit is a missionary Spirit. Over 300 years ago, that same Spirit also caused the extraordinary expansion of the Moravian missionary movement, which is one of the most powerful of such movements in Protestant mission history. Count Zinzendorf welcomed refugees to his farm in Herrnhut (in Germany today) who were believers from decidedly different backgrounds.

Because they were a diverse crowd, they experienced much disunity. However, on one Sunday in 1727, the Holy Spirit impacted them and melted the ice from their hearts, created harmony among them, and gave them a common vision for reaching those who had not yet heard the Gospel. These people proceeded to go to almost 30 different countries, giving a strong impetus to missions movements in Europe.[1]

At the beginning of the 20th century, people who encountered the Pentecostal experience at Azusa Street were filled with zeal to reach the world. Like the early Church and the Moravians, they too went to other countries as pioneer missionaries, or encouraged those who were already missionaries to be filled with the Holy Spirit.[2] That began the shift of the centre of gravity of Christendom to the Southern hemisphere. The character of the Pentecostal power is expansive.

The impact of the Spirit is not only needed by those who go; the senders also need that empowerment. Thus, we see the Holy Spirit speaking to the church in Antioch to send Paul and Barnabas as missionaries (Acts 13:1-4), inspiring the church at Ephesus through Paul's teaching ministry to reach the whole province of Asia (Acts 19:8-10), and causing the church of Thessalonica to become well-known for its activity in missions (I Thess. 1:8). Indeed, most of the New Testament churches were missions-oriented. Since the Holy Spirit always leads us to think of those who have never heard the Gospel, if a church is not missions-minded, something is wrong. Article 14 of the Lausanne Covenant expresses this very clearly: "A church that is not a missionary church is contradicting itself and quenching the Spirit."[3]

Every local and national church should carefully examine whether it is appropriately involved in God's plan to make Jesus known throughout the world. However, it's easy to see that not every church takes the Great Commission seriously. If each Pentecostal church provided one missionary, the world would experience a spiritual

---

[1]Ruth A. Tucker, *From Jerusalem to Irian Jaya* (Grand Rapids: Zondervan, 1983),70.

[2]Gary B. McGee, "Early Pentecostal Missionaries: They went Everywhere Preaching the Gospel", ed. Grant McClung, *Azusa Street and Beyond* (Alachua: Bridge.Logos, 2012), 35-40.

[3]Lausanne Covenant, article 14, 1974, https://www.lausanne.org/content/covenant/lausanne-covenant (Accessed February 20, 2017).

revolution. For instance, in Brazil, if every one of that nation's more than 10,000 local Pentecostal churches would send one missionary, the number of Brazilian Pentecostal missionaries would be about 10 times greater. In Finland, while Pentecostals do have about one missionary per local church, it is their dream to have one missionary per 100 church members.

Increasing the number of missionaries should be a matter of concern for every church. The senior or lead pastor, the elders, board of deacons (i.e., the leadership) must be committed to the missions vision of the church. Their attitude toward world missions is the indicator of the depth of spirituality in the church, because, again, the Holy Spirit is a missionary Spirit.

How the Spirit Works Through His Empowered People

Teaching (by Word and Example) Regarding the Centrality of Missions

The Holy Spirit is the Inspiring Breath of God, who instills in the Church a natural law, which is the instinctive desire to carry out evangelism and missions. "And Jesus came up and spoke to them, saying, 'All authority has been given to me in heaven and on earth. Go therefore and make disciples of all the nations, baptizing them in the name of the Father and the Son and the Holy Spirit, teaching them to observe all that I commanded you; and lo, I am with you always, even to the end of the age'" (Matt. 28:18-20). This Great Commission has a prominent place in the history of missions. It has given birth to many missionary movements and has spurred many Christians to commit their all on mission fields around the world.

William Carey (1761-1834), the father of the modern missionary movement, found his inspiration in the Great Commission. His tract, *An Enquiry into the Obligations of Christians to Use Means for the Conversion of the Heathen*, opposed the theology of his time—a theology that assumed that the Great Commission had expired with the first apostles.[4] Even Martin Luther had taught nothing else, saying

---

[4]Harry R. Boer, *Pentecost and Missions* (Grand Rapids: Eerdmans, 1961), 17.

"The Great Commission was exclusively for the first apostles, that they go everywhere and testify. After that, no-one else has received such a commission and every pastor has to care only for his own parish."[5] According to Luther, to personally accept this commission that the Lord Jesus gave his apostles, whereby a candidate would consider himself an equal to the first apostles, was an infringement, which also was the error of the Pope himself.[6]

Carey, however, brushed all those theological constructs aside. In Carey's day, Britain had begun to expand her rule, and for the first time something that is known today as "globalization" was experienced. Moreover, English and American churches not only survived the onslaught of the Enlightenment, but also experienced different revivals, which led to the Golden Age of Missions in the 19th century. Carey played a significant role in showing that the Church is still responsible to carry out the Great Commission.

The doyen of early German missiology, Gustav Warneck, wrote a book, *Evangelische Missionslehre* (*Evangelical Doctrine of Missions*). He researched the reason for modern missionary work and concluded that the main reason for its existence was that Christians took Matthew 28:18ff literally.[7] Even the rather recent beginning of Youth with a Mission (YWAM) goes back to Matthew 28; in his autobiography, founder Loren Cunningham states that he was compelled to start YWAM because of the Great Commission.[8]

However, when reading the New Testament, we see that Jesus' disciples did not immediately set to work after he had issued the Great Commission. Although hearing his words much stronger than anybody thereafter, they did not go right away. This was because Jesus gave them another commandment; he told them to wait (Luke 24:49). The first disciples, who later were called apostles, became the leaders and powerful witnesses of the emerging Church and missions movement

---

[5]*Martin Luther's Werke*, Kritische Gesamtausgabe (Critical Edition) (Weimar, Germany:Hermann Bohlaus Nachfolger, 1897), vol. 31, 210f.

[6]Andrew F. Walls, *The Missionary Movement in Christian History* (New York: Orbis Books, 2000), 246.

[7]Gustav Warneck, *Evangelische Missionslehre* (2. Aufl., Gotha, 1897), vol.1, 91.

[8]Loren Cunningham, *Is that Really You, God?* (Seattle: YWAM Publishing, 2001), chapter 4.

only after the outpouring of the Holy Spirit on the day of Pentecost. Everything that happened before Pentecost was like "ready . . . , steady . . . ," but the "GO" came only with the outpouring of the Holy Spirit. From that day forward, missionary work became the daily habit of the disciples—their lifestyle.

Although termed "the Great Commission," Matthew 28:18-20 is not actually a commission but rather an initial imperative known as a "natural law." What is a natural law? It's a decree given by God that corresponds with our being and our inherent fabric as human beings. That is why we like to follow natural laws. God decreed the natural laws during creation, and they are always given at the beginning of a person's existence.

Two such natural laws can be found in Genesis 1:28, which says, "God blessed them and said to them, 'Be fruitful and increase in number, fill the earth and subdue it. Rule over the fish of the sea and the birds of the air and over every living creature that moves on the ground.'" The first law seen here is the law of replenishment, and the second is the law to rule, which also has a lot to do with self-preservation. These two laws are so ingrained in us that we will carry them out without even knowing them. We can certainly agree that man has fulfilled both natural laws, since the earth is over-populated and the entire creation has been subdued under mankind.

However, these two laws were not the only ones given in the Garden of Eden, but two other distinct Spirit-filled moments occurred as well. The first was when God breathed living breath into man's body and so man became a living being. The second pneumatological moment came when God blessed the first human couple. Therefore, we find that a natural law is made up of two components: it comes through God's spoken Word and, connected to that decree, is an action by the Holy Spirit, who fills and blesses the recipients. These two events plant a natural law in the recipients, which can be expressed via the following formula: Commandment + Spirit = Natural Law.

The same components can be found in the New Testament. God decreed missions in Matthew 28, but on the day of Pentecost the Holy Spirit filled the believers and thus the Great Commission became the natural law of the Church. The New Testament church does not evangelize out of obedience, but by instinct. She is the Church only since Pentecost because her life principle—mission—was given to her on that same day.[9]

Luke writes that there were 120 people in the early-morning prayer meeting on the day of Pentecost. They had gathered and started praying, and then the Holy Spirit fell. There were tongues of fire, and people expressed their emotions to such a degree that bystanders thought they were drunk. The believers also spoke in tongues and prophesied. We don't know how long that prayer meeting lasted, but we do know who called this wonderful, charismatic moment to a halt and why. It was Peter! He noticed the unbelievers there and had the urge to tell them who this Jesus really was. I am afraid many congregations nowadays would have continued to carry on with worshipping and prophesying without noticing the unbelievers and telling them about Jesus. Yet Peter got up and preached a wonderful, clear-cut evangelistic sermon, and the result was that the hearers were convicted of their sin, repented, and were baptized. So, the Church started to grow in a phenomenal way.

It is spiritually healthy to realize that the charismata and the evangelism on the day of Pentecost constituted one inseparable effect of the Holy Spirit's outpouring. We are the ones who separate worship and evangelism by venues, times, or people responsible for it; but God sees them as one.

This natural law for believers (i.e., having the urge to tell others about Christ and, if it is cross-cultural, to do missions) was very well expressed by the first apostles. In fact, in Acts 4 we read that the apostles were interrogated by the Jewish leaders and then bluntly told to shut up. Peter's and John's answer to them is in Acts, verse 20: "We cannot but speak the things which we have seen and heard." In other words, even if they wanted to stop speaking about Christ, they couldn't. The Holy Spirit was simply bubbling over inside of them, and so, they spoke, witnessed, and preached.

Without the Holy Spirit, the Great Commission remains just a stiff law; but with the Spirit, it becomes the pulsating heartbeat of all church activities. The New Testament shows that the Church and missions

---

[9]Harry R. Boer, *Pentecost and Missions,* 63.

share the same birthday; after that, one cannot separate the two. Missions is not an independent enterprise; it's simply what the Church does. If the Church does not do missions any longer, then she ceases to be the Church in the full sense; and if mission becomes detached from the Church, then it will have lost its anchorage as well. Pentecost was the initial spark and full implementation of the Great Commission in and through the Church. The disciples did not testify about the risen Christ before Pentecost.[10]

We all were taught basic subjects in school, like mathematics and English. These subjects are so important that their absence would certainly have brought the entire school system into question. However, we also had extracurricular subjects. For me, one of elective was cooking; my daughters enjoy electives like drama, horseback-riding, and karate. Sometimes it seems that missions have now become an extracurricular activity in our churches. Some believers show an interest in foreign countries and other cultures, but as a whole the Church does not define herself through missions. Let me say it as clearly as I can: Evangelism and missions are constitutional for any church. Without the two, we cannot yet speak of a biblical Church in the same way that the New Testament does.

Overcoming Prejudice and Racism

Starting on the day of Pentecost, the Church became a kerygmatic fellowship, meaning that the body of believers lives from, and for, the proclamation of the risen Lord. As already seen, this kind of Spirit-filled Church needed no outside motivation to evangelize. However, the scope of its mission was not yet defined. Reading Acts, we can see how the Holy Spirit opened many doors for the Church to expand her mission.

Peter stood at the centre of this initial ministry because he had to fulfill Christ's prophecy that he received about the keys of the Kingdom of Heaven (Matt. 16:19). Keys are made for doors. Doors either lock up things or they can open rooms. Contrary to many jokes, Peter did

---

[10]Karl Barth, *Auslegung von Matthäus 28:16-2(*Basel, 1945), p. 8. quoted in Harry R. Boer, *Pentecost and Missions(* Grand Rapids: Eerdmans, 1961), 122.

not receive keys in order to admit or deny someone from entering heaven. So, for what kind of doors did he receive those keys? It was Peter who opened the way of salvation for the Jews first by preaching to them on the day of Pentecost. Again, it was Peter who first preached to the Gentiles in the house of the Roman officer, Cornelius. The key was the Gospel itself; but the doors were obstacles of prejudice, racism, segregation, and xenophobia. Some of those doors had been closed for centuries—until the Holy Spirit opened them.

It started on the day of Pentecost. There was an international gathering of Jews to celebrate the Day of Pentecost at the temple in Jerusalem. There were not yet, to the best of our knowledge, foreigners (non-Jews) involved, but one sign strongly pointed to the church's soon-to-begin mission. The believers were filled with the Holy Spirit and they spoke in foreign tongues. Now, speaking a foreign language is the essence of cross-culturalism. Here was, yet without encountering gentiles in face to face mission, a God-given sign to burst the seams of cultural particularism.

In Acts 3, we meet a man who had been paralyzed for years. While this made him an object of theological debate in his society, he never found any pity (not to mention healing). According to Levitical law, he was barred from attending the temple because of his condition. It was a hard lot for a Jewish man not to be counted as a full member of God's covenant people, yet he had a longing for God. The fact that he begged at the entrance to the temple not only speaks of his shrewdness when begging, but also of his longing to see, hear, and smell what was going on in the sanctuary.

Looking at Christ's ministry to people, we can conclude that to him nobody is an outsider. The apostles Peter and John continued with the same attitude. Upon being healed, this paralyzed man was integrated into God's covenant people. Now he was able to walk; in fact, he could jump! And where did he jump? Probably into the temple, because that was where the first church assembled. The Holy Spirit made it clear from that day forward that handicapped people are included in the assembly of God's children.

Acts 7 tells of Stephen, one of the prime movers in the New Testament. He was accused of blasphemy by the Jewish leaders and then stoned to death by a religious mob, while an ambitious Pharisee,

Saul of Tarsus, oversaw the carnage. Why was Stephen killed? Because the Spirit of God, who does not allow discrimination between people, had filled him and caused him to preach the truth. In exposing that discrimination, he abolished the notion of the Jews' special election, their temple, and their Law, presenting instead a God who loved all people regardless of their ethnic or religious background.

Saul became Stephen's "executioner" in a twofold sense. First, he oversaw the execution of the verdict against him; and second, after his conversion, Paul executed the spiritual legacy that Stephen had left. Not only had Stephen boldly proclaimed the love of God immediately before his death, but then he prayed that God would forgive his murderers. And my, how the Lord in his grace answered that prayer! For soon after, Jesus appeared to Saul on the road to Damascus, pushed him to the ground, and made him a new creation. This very Saul then lived for the message for which Stephen had died, carrying the Gospel into the streets, marketplaces, and palaces across the Roman Empire. Paul reflected his missionary work theologically in many passages of his writings. For example, in Colossians 1:26, he talks about a "great mystery"—that Jesus has abolished the separation between Jews and Gentiles (see also Ephesians 2:14).

Before Paul's conversion, we can see another racial barricade that was done away with by the Holy Spirit, for it is only he who can move people in a direction in which suddenly there is a willingness to reconcile. The Samaritans were reached by a deacon named Philip (see Acts 8). His task in the church had been to serve soup at the tables; in addition, he had an urge to tell others about Jesus. Seemingly, he had forgotten the violent history and civil wars between his people, the Jews, and the Samaritans. In fact, a pious Jew would go to bed with this prayer: "I thank thee, Lord, for not making me a woman, neither a pagan, nor a Samaritan, Amen" (in that order). The Samaritans, on the other hand, weren't saints either. There is a story that is told that once a bunch of Samaritans crept up to a Jewish town and threw a pig's carcass over the wall, in order to ritually defile the entire town.

Now the Holy Spirit confirmed God's plan for the Samaritans by working mighty signs and wonders in their midst through Philip. The Jewish Christians saw firsthand how God accepted Samaritans when the latter were baptized in the Holy Spirit. It is this sign that brings the breakthrough in reconciliation between people.   God made his approval of the Samaritans clear, now the Christians would have to follow his example and accept them too.

Philip was also involved in bringing the Gospel to someone with a different ethnicity. He met the Ethiopian chancellor and explained Christ to him by interpreting passages from the Old Testament. For whatever reason, this high-ranking political official had been drawn to the Jewish religion. However, the Jews would never regard him as belonging fully to them, both because of his different appearance, but mostly because he was a eunuch. Again, the Spirit of God commanded his servant to disregard racial prejudices and present the Gospel to this African. Immediately after he believed, Philip baptized him, showing that the body of Christ is open to all ethnicities. Philip's rapture from the scene of the Ethiopian's baptism further validated the Spirit's power, and confirmed God's plan of salvation for all.

The events at the house of the Roman officer, Cornelius, served to remove any remaining doubts concerning God's reconciliatory purpose for humankind. When the Spirit of God fell on Cornelius' household, we truly have a paradigm shift.[11] But first, let us consider some interesting background.

About 750 years earlier in a town called Joppa, God commanded the prophet Jonah to go warn the wicked city Nineveh of their immoral life-style and its consequences. At first, Jonah did not obey but he was brought to follow his calling through the entrails of a sea monster. Transporting involuntary missionaries in fish is not very practical, and so the Old Testament's record of missions to the unreached nations stops right there. It's said that Jonah "goes down" three times—first from his mountain village in Galilee to the coastal town of Joppa, then he went down into the ship, and last he went to hide deep in the ship so that nobody, including the God he was running from, could bother him. Centuries later, we find Simon bar Jonah (Peter) also in Joppa; the apostle is standing at the same junction of salvation history, in the very same place, Acts 9:43. This time, with the Holy Spirit and not out of sheer obedience, things work out better. Peter goes up to a rooftop

---

[11]Harry R. Boer, *Pentecost and Missions*, 75.

where he received a vision that went against the grain of his Jewishness: God commanded Peter to eat all kinds of "unclean" animals. God only took a fish to bring Jonah to Nineveh, but in order to bring Peter to the gentiles, he needed an entire zoo. Yet the difference here is the Holy Spirit, the one who drives people into missions and helps us to love those whom we would otherwise disregard. The Spirit drew upon a huge arsenal of spiritual means to bring Peter to the Gentiles: angels, visions, and gifts of the Spirit were all employed to prepare the apostle (and subsequently the Church) for this gigantic step.

Peter's journey continued from Joppa to Caesarea. Currently, it may be difficult to imagine how many obstacles of hate, prejudice, and racism Peter stepped over that day when he entered Cornelius' house. Cornelius wasn't just a Gentile, but a Roman. He was a citizen of the invading country that cruelly oppressed the Jews. In addition, he wasn't just a Roman, but a soldier who likely had led his men into combat against the Jews. Yet Peter, knowing that he was led by the Spirit of God, commenced to do what by that time certainly had become routine to him. He talked about Jesus, and continued doing so, until interrupted by the Holy Spirit. Since there was only divine order in that meeting, it's almost as if you could hear Jesus shouting from heaven, "I cannot wait any longer!" Jesus baptized Cornelius and his entire household in the Holy Spirit; this happened before they were baptized in water. Acts 10:44-46 says that they were filled, prophesied, and spoke in tongues—a mighty chorus of praise ringing out from the mouths of "untouchables"!

Having witnessed God in action, Peter later reported these events to the other apostles. The apostles' deliberations were no longer of a spiritual nature. They talked about the cultural implications of what God himself had spiritually made clear (Acts 15, 19ff). From that day forward, the church resolved to be a reconciled body of believers from all walks of life, all languages, and all ethnicities. The core of the Holy Spirit's work among people is to bring such a church into existence—up to this very day.

Bringing About Reconciliation

In his famous interpretation of the Holy Spirit's work in Church history, Kenneth Scott Latourette reasoned that Christianity advances through revivals. One can readily see in many of those revivals that barriers of prejudice, sexism, racism, and ageism were torn down, at least for a while. The Azusa Street Revival, which started in 1906, is a prime example of such a move of the Spirit. There the "*color bar was washed away*" in the blood of Christ; children preached; black "laundry ladies" prophesied;[12] and single ladies were sent out as missionaries. William F. Seymour, the son of former slaves, laid hands on white Lutheran bishops who had sailed over from Europe. For many years, one could witness the wonderful breakdown of discriminatory structures prevalent in the society of that day. Other parallel instances in church history come to mind, and two such examples are St. Patrick, and A.B. Simpson.

St. Patrick, founder of the Celtic Church in Ireland in the 5th century, was a strong opponent of slavery. Somebody once said that, until the 17th century, there was no one else who had so solid a stand against slavery as St. Patrick.[13] Where did his attitude come from? It is interesting that Patrick's ministry, and that of the Celtic Church in general, were characterized by signs and wonders. Patrick was one of the last men before the Middle Ages whom we would call "Pentecostal." That's why the Pentecostal churches in Ireland still claim his ministry as such an important part of their heritage. We can learn from Patrick's example how charismatic ministry goes together with the absence of prejudice.

A.B. Simpson, one of the spiritual trailblazers of the modern Pentecostal Movement, ministered especially in missions and faith healing.[14] At the end of the 19th century, his church was known to be the most modern and richest congregation in New York City. But when Simpson led hundreds of Italian migrants for Christ, his church

---

[12]Frank Bartleman, *How Pentecost came to Los Angeles*, Plainfield, New Jersey: Logos International, 1980, 32.

[13]David Carnduff, *Ireland's Lost Heritage,* Portadown: IPBC Publications, 2003), 9.

[14]Charles Nienkirchen, "Simpson, Albert Benjamin," in: Stanley M. Burgess, ed., *The New International Dictionary of Pentecostal and Charismatic Movements*, Grand Rapids: Zondervan, 2003, 1069f.

members (including the church elders) refused to accept them in their midst. Thereupon, despite the pleading of colleagues and his own wife, and to the amazement of the press, Simpson resigned his pastorate. And although he became independent, he advised his most faithful church members not to follow him, but to remain in the church. It took only ten years to see that the Lord had more than rewarded his servant. Simpson built and shepherded another strong congregation, moved into an international ministry, became one of the most famous faith healers in the USA, and his missions board supported 24 missionaries around the globe.

Conveying Love as the Key Ingredient in Missions

It is impossible to be Pentecostal and racist at the same time. While much has been discussed and written regarding the "initial evidence" of the baptism in the Holy Spirit, the Word of God makes it abundantly clear what the strongest evidence of the Spirit's infilling is: love. Paul said, ". . . because the love of God has been poured out within our hearts through the Holy Spirit who was given to us" (Rom. 5:5). When we are filled with the Spirit, it means that we will have more love than we would otherwise naturally have. In our own nature, we possess a limited amount of love, and it usually extends to a limited number of people, such as our children, our spouse, close relatives. And even that kind of love is not at its best all the time. Now, with the baptism in the Holy Spirit comes more love—a lot more—enabling us to love people who would usually be out of our scope to love. Luke 6:32-35f says, "If you love those who love you, what credit is that to you? For even sinners love those who love them . . . But love your enemies, and do good . . . Be merciful, just as your Father is merciful." Mission is actually the amazing ability to love people we don't even know yet.

Jonah serves again in contrast to this. Throughout the book of Jonah, the Lord tried to teach him the most elementary lesson for missions work: to love, and feel compassion towards the Ninevites. God's mission education program for Jonah is summed up in the last verse of the book (4:11), the Lord saying, "Should I not have compassion on Nineveh, the great city in which there are more than 120,000 persons who do not know the difference between their right and left hand, as well as many animals?" Jonah did not affirm this question, for he felt nothing for the people. Neither did he have compassion for animals. So, the Lord had to teach him an even more basis lesson. "Okay, Jonah, you don't feel for people nor animals. So, let's start with a plant." And that worked! Jonah had compassion for the plant; and the Lord used it as an object lesson to show that his compassion extends to all people, even to Jonah's enemies, the Assyrians.

In the 1990s, I (Ulf) was invited to speak at a Bible school in South Africa. I was available only for one day, so they gathered all students from four classes in the chapel. When I got ready to go up and teach, I was startled to see the 100 assembled students. So, I asked the principal, "I know your churches and that you have black congregations, too. So, how come you only have white students here?" He answered, "Our church has four Bible schools." It turned out that they had one for blacks, one for whites, one for coloureds, and one for those of Indian descent. Here they were, Pentecostals expecting the Holy Spirit to move in their lives and ministries, yet they discriminated in the use of the Spirit. They couldn't see the forest for the trees. Fortunately, they abandoned that system a short time later. "If I speak with the tongues of men and of angels, but do not have love, I have become a noisy gong or a clanging cymbal. If I have the gift of prophecy and know all mysteries and all knowledge; and if I have all faith so as to remove mountains but do not have love, I am nothing" (1 Corinthians 13:1-2f).

The Spirit of God deals with all of humanity, not just a part of it. He was there at creation as the living breath, the one who gives life to all. Pentecost was another milestone where we find the Holy Spirit working universally because he opened the door of salvation through Christ to all peoples and nations. He gave life in both instances—at creation and again at Pentecost. Thus, the outpouring at Pentecost contrasts with the confusion of tongues at Babylon, for the Spirit never splits people apart; he reconciles them.

Equipping Others to Carry Out the Missions Mandate

Spiritual gifts assured to those who spread the Gospel

In Matthew 28:19-20, Jesus issued his Great Commission to the disciples, followed by the promise, "And surely I am with you always . . ." From the context, it's clear that the promise was meant especially for those who carry out the Great Commission mandate. In other words, one needs to implement the first part to be able to claim the second part. I know that there are people who seem to experience the "presence of God" when finding a parking space in an overcrowded mall. Yet, interpreting the context of Matthew 28, I think this promise is more for those who talk boldly about Christ in their Muslim community, or those who carry Bibles into countries where doing so is unlawful and punishable with jail sentences.

The danger with Christianity is for it to turn inward. Some people exercise the gifts of the Spirit as if entertaining themselves on a charismatic playground. It is certainly true that God wants to work miracles in our midst, and that we do not see as many healings as we should in our churches. Yet, can we assume that when the Holy Spirit creates a perfect church no one is ever sick and no funerals take place? Is that an ideal that's been thought through? The emphasis of the Spirit's work in the New Testament was outward. The Spirit wants to work inside our churches, yes, but his main thrust is outward. Miracles happened on the streets as Christians engaged in evangelism; and powerful gifts supported the mission expansion of the Church.

The value of accompanying "Signs"

The Gospel of Mark paints a clear picture of how God ranks spiritual gifts, "These signs will accompany those who have believed: in My name they will cast out demons, they will speak with new tongues; they will pick up serpents, and if they drink any deadly poison, it will not hurt them; they will lay hands on the sick, and they will recover" (16:17-18). Just as in Matthew 28, this promise of the Spirit's supernatural presence is bound to the Great Commission, as shown in Mark 16:15.

The word "accompany" was used in antiquity when talking about parades. Different kinds of parades took place, such as a victory parade or when a king rode into town. Accompanying him were his courtiers, ministers, generals, sentries, the queen with her maids, and yes, kings had fools, too. Doubtless the masses were fascinated with such a display of grandeur and nobility. The people were likely in awe of the soldiers and dazzled by the finest fashion paraded in front of them. Yet, the unmistakable centre of all attention was the king himself. People stood on their tiptoes or climbed into trees to catch a glimpse of the monarch.

The same must be said about the gifts of the Spirit. The gifts of the Spirit accompany our king and are part and parcel of what happens when God moves into town. Spiritual gifts certainly hold a fascination on their own, yet they should never distract from, but rather point to, Christ. The early Pentecostals had novel, and in some cases, abundant experiences with the supernatural workings of the Holy Spirit; yet those experiences were at the same time absolutely Christ-centered. They had a phrase that expresses this point well: "Do not seek the gift, but seek the giver!"

The fruit of the Spirit

Before we turn to power and miracles, it is worth noting that the fruit of the Spirit, listed in Galatians 5:22-23, also play a vital role in evangelism and missionary work. The first fruit mentioned is, of course, love. Some commentators interpret that to mean the fruit is only love. They see the other eight fruit of the Spirit (joy, peace, patience, kindness, goodness, faithfulness, gentleness, and self-control) as aspects, or ingredients, of love. This speaks of the fact that the word "fruit" in verse 22 is in the singular mode. In that case, we do not have different fruits of the Spirit, like a colourful fruit basket in front of us, but only one fruit (say, a grape) which has different arms. This very neatly falls in line with what I have written previously, namely that the Holy Spirit fills our lives with love, and that this kind of love gives us compassion for the lost and spurs the believer onward to share the Gospel.

The fruit of the Spirit are not to be confined to inner sanctification. One quality of fruit is its attractiveness. Just the look of a juicy mango can make your mouth water. Likewise, the Holy Spirit works on the character qualities of believers so that others are drawn to us. This is an effect which has been very instrumental in evangelism. People notice something different about Christians. Their loving behaviour make a difference in schools and in factories. Christians are oftentimes able to comfort others during life-threatening dangers; and this, in turn, leads people to ask more about Jesus.

The roles of both natural and supernatural gifts

People often ascribe greater value to the supernatural gifts listed in 1 Corinthians 12:8ff over a person's natural gifts. "Natural" means our inherited qualities—e.g., that people are musical or are gifted communicators, or have leadership abilities. Some fancy to "only serve the Lord in the Spirit" and thus look down on natural faculties. So where do our natural abilities come from? They are passed on from generation to generation, a long chain which points back to creation. It is none other than the Holy Spirit who has endowed mankind with natural gifts. Thus, both supernatural and natural gifts have the same source—the Spirit.

I do not know whether carnal people can exercise spiritual gifts, but the story of Israel's physically strongest judge Samson, and the events in Corinth seem to suggest this. I do know that we can operate our natural gifts in a spiritual way. Case in point: I had an elderly lady in my church in Germany who had the gift of baking cakes. It was a wonderful ability, and I wish there were more people like her in our churches. Anyway, we planted a church in former East Germany, and many came to our meetings because this dear sister accompanied me every time I preached there, and she always brought cakes along. Admittedly, the people came for her cakes, not to hear me speak. But for some, this sweet gift opened the way for them to hear the Gospel and to eventually accept Christ into their lives.

In the realm of missions, all our faculties are to be employed for the glory of Christ. We need teachers, pastors, preachers, prophets; but we also need nurses, builders, painters, potato farmers, and administrators. Today, some countries cannot be entered by career missionaries, whereas people who can help develop businesses, technical industries, etc. are welcome.

The importance of "power evangelism"

If you are set to bring the Gospel to unbelieving relatives, or if you want to be a witness for Christ in your neighbourhood, or if you are ready to start a new church, then expect God to support your testimony with supernatural signs. Be bold and pray for miracles to occur. Sharing the Gospel is the prime operating field for the Holy Spirit who leads to breakthroughs in our ministries.

Also count on God to operate in negative situations as well as positive circumstances, believing that he will remove obstacles by supernatural intervention. For example, we see such miraculous interventions in Acts 13:8ff when Elymas the magician was blinded because he opposed the spread of the Gospel. Also, in the 5th century assassins targeted St. Patrick. In the instance of St. Patrick, the plot came to naught because all of the attackers were struck with dumbness (literally made speechless) in front of this man of God.[15] I am not implying that we go around striking or cursing people, but I am saying that missionaries who experience many obstacles as they are spreading the Gospel, can trust the Lord to clear the way.

There are manifold reasons why believers of other religions become Christians. For example, to Muslims, assurance of salvation seems to be one of the most attractive aspects of our faith. Yet I know of many instances when Jesus healed someone in a Muslim family, which then led to inquiry and, ultimately, to salvation. Another example is when pastors in Germany baptize former Muslims who have come to Europe as refugees, oftentimes seeking escape from an all-too-literal form of Islam. Many of these new believers are also baptized in the Holy Spirit right at the beginning of their Christian walk. What a joy it is to see how they, in turn, lay hands on the sick, the Lord working with and through them.

---

[15] Ibid.

Prophesy is another gift of the Spirit that can lead to breakthroughs in this area, something which religious debate will never accomplish. Encouraging cases come to mind from Iraq and Indonesia, where people encounter the living God who speaks directly into their lives.

I (Ulf) conclude this section on "How the Spirit Works Through His Empowered People" with this memory from Malawi in southeast Africa, where our family served as missionaries for 15 years. In 1998, I visited a local Pentecostal congregation in a village called Kaulira in the northern part of Malawi for the first time.[16] Entering the church on a Sunday morning, I was amazed to see 700 people assembled, which was perhaps more than the village's entire population. At the end of the service I could not help but ask the pastor why he had such a large congregation. He led me to two old men who were chatting with others outside the building and the pastor introduced me to Chekha Kumwenda and Kankhwala Banda.

The church in Kaulira had its beginnings in the late 1940s. No missionary had brought the Gospel to them. At that time, many Malawian men migrated to South Africa to work as miners, cooks, "house boys," etc. A goodly number of them found Christ on the streets of Johannesburg and in the mining compounds. Many workers suffered from tuberculosis; but word got around that Pentecostal preachers offered healing in the name of Jesus. Many people received not only that healing, but salvation as well. Upon their return to Malawi, these migrant "preachers" became missionaries to their home folks in Kaulira. Thus, around 1951, there was a small group of Christians in Kaulira who were barely literate but acquainted with the supernatural power of God.

One day, an accident in the village claimed the lives of two teenage boys. As was the custom, the corpses were laid in state in a hut, so that relatives and friends could pay their last respects. That small group of Christians entered the hut too, started singing some of their songs and then prayed over the dead bodies. Suddenly, both teenagers came back to life.

---

[16]Ulf Strohbehn, *Pentecostalism in Malawi, A History of the Apostolic Faith Mission* (Zomba: Kachere, 2002), 153.

Chekha Kumwenda and Kankhwala Banda, who stood with us outside the church in 1998, were those two boys who had been raised from the dead. They were already elderly when I met them. Nevertheless, whenever there were people in the meetings who had not yet received Christ, these two would go up to the pulpit and share their testimony with salvific effects! Our wonderful, life-giving God and his son Jesus Christ, together with the Holy Spirit, encourage us to have faith and exercise it in the supernatural—for the sake of his Kingdom and Glory.

Missions Strategy

Why is strategy so important? If we want to achieve results in anything we do, we need goals. An athlete needs the desire to win, to set a record; a business person aspires to become a market leader; a composer or artist wants to create top-rate productions. Originally, the word "strategy" was related to war; it was simply the answer to "How do we win the war?"

Jesus has given us a goal via his Great Commission—to reach all people everywhere with the Gospel. Strategy is the mapping out of how that goal is to be reached. Every church and every believer who is aware of what Jesus has done to save them from eternal condemnation must ask how they are to participate in the spread of the Gospel.

Unfortunately, many churches have never asked themselves what the Holy Spirit is directing them to do to fulfill the Great Commission, never asked where it is that God wants them to spread the Gospel, never asked how many missionaries he would have them support, never found (or even sought to find) their own Paul and Barnabas, never experienced being partners with the Holy Spirit in sending people. Missions must have a human face; but some churches want to "outsource" missions by just sending money, which is easier than praying that the Lord would call persons from their church to go, than investing in their training and committing to their long-term support.

If a church has a clear missions strategy (i.e., a plan for involvement in fulfilling the Great Commission), then every member of that church should know the goals and how they are to be accomplished. Some people may think that devising a strategy is in opposition to the spontaneous leading of the Holy Spirit. In certain cases that may be, but a correct understanding of strategy in the context of missions means an even deeper dependence on the Spirit. To understand the Lord's desire and plan concerning the church and individual believers forces us to seek the mind of God and the will of the Holy Spirit.[17]

The basic components of strategy consist of mission, vision, values, principles, and success factors, then setting out goals and the process, or means, to reach those goals. In order to reach those goals requires understanding and supporting the activities that will accomplish them. *Mission* is simply defined as the main task of the church (i.e., why the church exists). *Vision* describes how we want the future to look. *Values* will direct our decision-making, for we must analyze what is important for our consideration and which biblical values relate decisively to missionary work. *Principles* form our policies, the "how" we do missions work and which principles are followed in a practical sense. *Success factors* define the keys for measuring achievement; for example, we ask whether we can be successful without prayer.

Goals and sub-goals (objectives) inspire us and keep us on the right track. We follow Paul's example, who said, "Therefore I do not run aimlessly; I do not fight like a boxer beating the air" (1 Cor. 9:26). To reach the goals requires activities and processes. If we want to spread the Gospel, we need to be witnesses, to preach, to teach, to love our neighbours—to serve the "whole" person.

Lastly, it is important that we also focus on the support processes. These include leadership, information and marketing activities, human resource management, collecting funds, and financial oversight and reporting. It is often the case that some or all these areas are neglected, or at least underdeveloped. For example, leadership is vaguely designated, information-sharing sparse, missionaries not served properly, fund-raising unsystematic, and/or financial reporting is either lacking or defective. In beginning a missions movement, it is important to give proper and adequate consideration to all these

---

[17]Arto Hämäläinen, *How to Start Missionary Work in New Sending Countries* (Helsinki: FIDA International, 2003), 17.

practical issues. Too many missions endeavours suffer because of poor management. Paul praised the church at Philippi for their quality of management (Phil. 4:15-19). All missions organizations need to strive for high quality.

Antioch Church as a Model for Missions Strategy

The local church at Jerusalem was a bit slow in fulfilling the missions task. It was mono-cultural—i.e., it initially focused on reaching only the Jews. Gradually, however, it remembered Jesus' instructions to go beyond Jerusalem and Judea. Its first missionary to cross the cultural and religious borders was deacon/evangelist Philip, who, driven by persecution, went to Samaria (Acts 8:4ff). He subsequently crossed another border when he witnessed to the Ethiopian eunuch (Acts 8:27ff).

Not long after the events in Samaria and with the Ethiopian eunuch, again because of persecution, the Jerusalem church became a catalyst for cross-cultural missions at Antioch. Those tentmakers, or lay workers, who went to Antioch shared the Gospel with the Gentiles there (Acts 11:19-21). Barnabas and Lucius who also helped lay the foundation for the Antioch church had cross-cultural experience, having lived in Cyprus and Cyrene respectively. Thus, the believers in Antioch understood that they should not just be receivers of the message, but also become givers. Although blessed by the church in Jerusalem, they did not remain dependent on that church. Since giving is a divine principle (God gave his best, his begotten Son, Jesus Christ), the Antioch church grasped the concept as well. When the Jerusalem church faced a difficult time because of a famine (Acts 11:27-30), the "receivers" at Antioch became a "360-degree church."

The Antioch church not only gave humanitarian assistance to the church in Jerusalem, it began to send missionaries. We clearly see the guidance of the Holy Spirit in the sending out of Paul and Barnabas (Acts 13:1-4). Note that the Spirit "spoke" when the church leaders were praying and fasting. While we cannot force the Spirit to speak, we can provide a forum for him through fasting and prayer. Like Antioch, most of the New Testament churches became missionary-sending churches. They were 360-degree churches, not "90- or 180-

degree churches" with little interest and occasional input into missions. They understood their responsibility to be the agents for the fulfilling of the Great Commission. They had a clear understanding of the reason for their existence, which included not only to serve the personal needs of the believers in a centripetal way, but also to be centrifugal in sending people.

We can learn much about the missions strategy of Paul from the church in Antioch, and other churches with whom he was cooperating. First, we notice that Paul had *spiritual goals*. In Romans 15 he shared his vision of preparing the Gentiles as an offering to God (vv. 15-16). At the time of harvest, the Jews brought crops to the temple, which the priests then offered to God. Paul seemed to be thinking of this analogy. Pentecost was also a "harvest feast," and much symbolism is included in the fact that, at the first Pentecostal outpouring, people from many nations became believers and were filled with the Holy Spirit (Acts 2). Paul's desire was to bring that kind of offering to God from everywhere.

Second, Paul had *ethnic goals*. He crossed racial and ethnic borders. He was a Jew to the Jews (1 Cor. 9:20) but was also obligated to the Greeks and non-Greeks (Rom. 1:14). He had the attitude of a slave who must serve (i.e., win) as many as possible (1 Cor. 9:19). Paul saw that Jesus wants to redeem everyone, for "There is neither Jew nor Gentile, neither slave nor free, nor is there male and female, for you are all one in Christ Jesus" (Gal 3:28). Only through the atonement can we realize that all people are equal—all are sinners; therefore, everyone needs redemption by the blood of Jesus. That is the only lasting foundation for the egalitarian approach.

Third, Paul had *geographic goals* (Rom. 15:19-24). He had reached Illyricum (approximately Albania today), but he desired to expand his ministry to Rome and even Spain. Missions must be geographically oriented.

Fourth, Paul had *tactical goals*. He wanted to establish local churches everywhere. It was not enough for him to preach the Gospel, he wanted to leave the influence of the Church in every place he preached. The Church would be a centre of training, equipping, and multiplying. Jesus' command was to make disciples; so, to achieve that, the existence of the Church is a necessity. Disciples cannot grow in a vacuum.

Paul deemed it important that the church understand its role in a holistic way. The spiritual needs of people should, of course, be served, but they have other needs as well. In his letter to Titus, Paul often emphasized that the Church be ready to do good works (2:7, 14; 3:1, 8, 14). Loving our neighbour was a part of Jesus' message, reminding us to keep a balance between our love for God and love for our neighbour. The churches that Paul established became interconnected. Unity and cooperation are a reflection of the divine oneness (John 17). The New Testament churches were not independent, they were interdependent.

Structure to Implement the Missions Strategy

Any strategy is useless if there is no proper structure to implement it—like a piece of music on paper but without an instrument to play it. Pentecostals have created various kinds of structures for their national and local churches. Among them are those who influence missions. When they consider missions structures, new senders have crucial questions to ask. Among them are these: What is the national church's missions structure? What is the local church's missions structure? How are the national and local structures related? Which decisions are made on the national level and on the local level? How does the national structure network with continental and global mission structures?

Why is the structure needed? First, it must motivate people, recruiting them for missions. Second, the structure must provide training for both those who are sent and those who are sending. Third, sending people means providing a structure for accomplishing the goals of missions. Fourth, since the missionary or the missions organization are rarely alone in a country or an area, they need a format for partnering with others.

Antioch Church and Paul's Team as Models of Missions Structure

In the New Testament, local churches formed the basis for mission activities. In Acts 13, we see that the Holy Spirit cast the mission vision to the churches' leadership, who understood the instructions he gave.

Without the leadership 's involvement in the vision, it is almost impossible to move forward. In larger churches, the leadership can delegate practical implementation to a missions committee or task force. However, in every case, the responsibilities should be clearly spelled out. The missionary must know how decisions in the home church are made and what role it has in the whole picture.

One might be tempted to say that a missions organization has no model in the New Testament, but that is not necessarily so. Although we cannot find it described in modern terms, nonetheless the "embryo" is detectable. If we follow Paul and his team on their journeys, we notice that they did not communicate with Antioch about everything. They reported back to the home church, but they did not consult with the home church about every decision. The team usually made decisions along the way. For instance, when the Holy Spirit hindered their going to Asia Minor or Bithynia (Acts 16:6-7), or when the Spirit spoke to Paul in a vision about going to Europe, the final decision rested with Paul and his team (Acts 16:8-10). Would they obey the Spirit's leading? Some of them may have had their doubts, but they made the decision to follow the Spirit.

We also see that the local church made some decisions (e.g., the sending and supporting of Paul and Barnabas) and partly by Paul and his team. Paul and his team typically made decisions for situations that arose on the field. For example, Antioch had no real idea of the situation in the centre of today's Turkey. Decision-making required some expertise, and Paul with his team were fully able to provide that expertise. Here then we see that Paul's team were the embryo of a missions organization or missions department for a national church. When it comes to decision-making in world missions, we need input from both the local church and the national church. It is important to define the roles of both. We must decide which matters are to be decided on the local level and which at the national level.

It is also essential to decide how a national church, through its missions department or missions organization, will partner with other missions entities. If it is connected to continental and/or global mission organizations, that can be a big help. Then the missionaries who are sent out can likewise be connected to other missionaries working in the same area and/or focusing on the same people group. Our testimony thus becomes stronger, and we can utilize the best practices tested by others.

Questions for Reflection

What is the mission vision of my church? Does my church have a missions strategy? Is there a missions structure in my church? Is the relationship between the local church and national church clearly defined? What can we learn from New Testament churches regarding world missions?

Chapter 2

Purposes for Structure

Missions need four basic elements for implementing a mission program. Those elements are as follows: (1) mobilizing and recruiting people (who?); (2) training people (what, how?); (3) sending the missionaries (by whom, to where?); and (4) partnering with others (with whom?).

Aspects of Mobilizing and Recruiting

Mobilizing and Recruiting People for Ministry and Missions

We must first answer the question as to who will meet the need. Missions is about people. Jesus' command was that we ask God to send workers into the harvest (Matt. 9:38). We need others not just the "goers." In other words, it is a mistake to concentrate only on the missionaries, for "How can anyone preach [i.e., go] unless they are sent?" (Rom. 10:15). Thus, we need people who recognize their calling as "senders." We must mobilize them to first understand, and then successfully accomplish, their role.

We need tools for motivating and recruiting these senders. One of the best such tools is the international Kairos Course. It has been powerfully effective in igniting a vision for world missions in local churches.[1] It was started in the Philippines in 1994, and has since spread all over the world and in many different languages. Today some 100 countries use this course. Following is one example of its impact.

The course greatly blessed a Finnish missionary couple, and they began to teach it in their country of Uganda, inspiring many people. Among them were four young students, who told the couple they could not remain silent while knowing that in northern Uganda lived 200,000 refugees from Sudan, including many from unreached people groups. Subsequently, this team of students made four trips to one of the refugee camps, followed by a trip to Sudan.

As churches learn about world missions through the "*Kairos* Course," or other means, they need to provide forums in which people called by God to go can hear the Holy Spirit speaking to them (as was the case of the young Ugandans). Nobody will investigate the possibility of going if their church never has a missions event, or if they do not have the opportunity to hear a missions message. What Paul writes is "trust" when he says that "Faith comes from hearing the message, and the message is heard through the word about Christ" (Rom. 10:17). Pastors need to preach about world missions if they want to see their people get involved. Pastors must inspire them to pray for workers, for missionaries. In Finland, we prayed to add 100 more missionaries in five years' time. God gave that number in just four years—proof that our prayer was pleasing to him.[2]

Mobilization will often start with small steps. To illustrate, I visited Czechoslovakia during the communist era. At that time, Pentecostal churches were illegal, and it was risky to contact them. Gathering at remote places in mountainous areas, I experienced a baptismal service in the moonlight and people finding Jesus as their Saviour. I spoke to the believers about world missions, although they could not leave for any field as missionaries. However, they were creative in their missions vision. They wanted to pray for world missions, so they asked for the names of our Finnish missionaries to

---

[1] More information about the Kairos course can be found at the website www.simplymobilizing.com

[2] Arto Hämäläinen, *How to Start Missionary Work in New Sending Countries* (Helsinki: FIDA International, 2003), 21.

add to their prayer list. We learned a few years later (when the Iron Curtain came down) that these prayers met some of these missionaries face to face. Then they started to send their own missionaries to at least eight different countries. These missionaries worked among the unreached people groups in Central Asia and the Middle East.

The Barnabas Principle

The first mission society had one significant aspect that served as the foundation for its structure. At the core of its organization were the relationships among key people. I don't mean relationships in general but rather a special kind— "spiritual parenthood." Mentors ushered apostles, leaders, and missionaries into the ministry.

During the New Testament era, mature Christians functioned as spiritual midwives and parents to younger or newer believers. Even though Paul's letters contained designations for offices like elder, deacon, overseer, and apostle, he nonetheless implied that he was a spiritual father and even like a spiritual mother (see 1 Tim. 1:2, Gal. 4:19). The letters of John used these kinds of titles in the church— children, young men, fathers. The principle of spiritual parenthood was so strong in the first churches that it was only natural to speak of their religious officers as family members.[3]

Paul was the product of the leaders who taught him, three of whom we can readily identify. *Gamaliel* was Paul's theological teacher who certainly had given him a thorough grounding in the Scriptures, but this even was before he met Christ. While Paul's conversion was "heavenly," his subsequent training was very much "down to earth." His spiritual father was *Ananias,* who helped this broken, blinded man onto the path of discipleship. Ananias laid hands on Paul and prayed he would regain his sight and receive the Holy Spirit. Then, Ananias baptized him in water. Ananias was also significant because he was the first one to call Paul "brother," and thus he opened the door for this former persecutor's acceptance in the churches. When we compare

---

[3] "It is less well known that *neōteros* . . . [young men] serves as a designation for junior church officers, equivalent to *diakonos*." Raymond E. Brown, *The Epistles of John* (New Haven: Yale University Press, 1982), 299.

these events described in Acts 9 with the opening paragraph of Acts 19, we see a pattern emerging. In the former, Paul was mentored; whereas in the latter, he mentored others and helped people the same way that others had helped him—i.e., laying hands on them, and baptizing them in water. Last, while Ananias helped Paul to become a Christian, a third figure emerged—*Barnabas*, who helped move Paul into the ministry. We certainly can learn much from the man credited with "producing a Paul," including the following ministry-development principles.

Barnabas believed in people

The Bible first mentioned Barnabas in Acts 4:36. This was already very telling, because the apostles, observing this Joseph, called him by a name they had coined especially for him— "son of encouragement," which is the literal meaning of Barnabas. He indeed was an encourager, causing people to feel better after meeting him and giving hope to the downcast. He did not function as a spiritual policeman, ready to find fault. Rather, he seemed to be always on the lookout for traits in people through which he could spur them onward. Barnabas saw potential that often remained obscure to others. He already saw promise in Paul when everyone else was still afraid of the man. He introduced Paul to the apostles (Acts 9:27) and made a case for him. Regarding young John Mark (Acts 15:36ff), we see that Barnabas was willing to give people a second chance.

Jerry Cook tells a story about a couple that went fishing.[4] The wife, who had been taught how to fish, was looking forward to landing a big catch. Boarding a fishing boat, they went out onto the ocean and threw their baited hooks into the water. Soon, the wife felt a strong tug on her line. As she began to reel in her catch, one of the ship's crew took the rod out of her hand and proceeded to land her fish, which turned out to be a small shark. The crewman might have meant well by helping the woman, but she was very disappointed about his assistance. She wanted to land the catch herself, she felt betrayed,

---

[4]Jerry Cook, *Love, Acceptance and Forgiveness* (Bloomington: Bethany House, 2009), 72f.

robbed of her moment to shine. She had trained for it, but the crew member denied her the final triumph.

Now imagine Barnabas being on that boat! He would not have taken the rod from the woman's hand. Instead, he would have stood next to her, perhaps instructing her a bit and certainly would have congratulated her for catching such a prize on her own. Encouragers bring people into the ministry by trusting them. They know when to pull back so that others can shine.

Barnabas shared his ministry

Barnabas was a generous person. He was part and parcel of that generous attitude which characterized the Jerusalem church (Acts 4:32ff). He owned a piece of land (probably around Jerusalem) that his family kept as an inheritance, yet he sold it for the benefit of the poorer members in the church (v. 34).

Another dimension of sharing also characterizes Barnabas. A member of the tribe of Levi, he was thus of priestly descent. Originally from the island of Cyprus, he would have travelled once a year to Jerusalem to perform his duties at the temple, a ministry that lasted for about two weeks each year.[5] The Levites were grouped into teams to care for the animals to be sacrificed, perform sacrifices, counsel people, read the Scriptures publicly, and help maintain the sanctuary. All this might have contributed to Barnabas becoming a believer in the first place. Many priests became followers of Jesus in those days because they "saw" Christ in the performance of their daily duties, e.g., when sacrificing the animals (Acts 6:7).

Thus, even before he became a follower of Jesus, Barnabas learned to serve in a team. Team ministry implies two basic lessons and both are vital for success in the ministry: (1) Each person is responsible to do their part, otherwise the mission of the entire team is in danger. (2) No one can do everything on their own; they need others to complement their ministry.

---

[5]Frédéric Godet, *Kommentar zu dem Evangelium des Lukas* (Giessen: Brunnen, 1986), 54f.

An article describes two elderly women, Margaret Patrick and Ruth Eisenberg, who were residents of the Southeast Senior Center for Independent Living in Englewood, New Jersey, USA.[6] Both women were accomplished pianists, each had spent much of her life-giving lessons to aspiring children. In 1982, both women suffered crippling strokes. Margaret barely survived. After spending months in hospitals and rehabilitation facilities, she finally regained movement on her left side; however, her right side remained paralyzed. With halting speech, she often said, "I am happy to be alive." Ruth, who has a wisecracking wit, laughed about the moment when she suffered her stroke and laid on the floor of her apartment undiscovered for two days. Although she recovered, she did not have the use of her left side and she was confined to a wheelchair.

The two women met after their doctors referred them both to the independent living centre by their doctors, and they soon learned of their mutual love for the piano. One day, they sat down at the centre's ancient piano. Margaret's long fingers moved back and forth over the left side of the keyboard, while Ruth's shorter, stronger fingers carried the melody on the right side. They sat close together and leaned toward one another; Margaret's right hand draped limply around Ruth, and Ruth's left hand laid motionless on Margaret's right knee. Their first attempt, Chopin's "Minute Waltz in D," was truly a revelation to both. Since then they have developed an extensive repertoire, performing at countless senior centres, veteran's homes, and hospitals. They were even featured on television shows. They are an inspiration to all who hear them play. Says Margaret, "I never thought God could use us the way he is doing. We are so happy, and we thank God every day." After their strokes, neither of these women could play challenging music by herself, but working as a team they performed beautiful music.

Barnabas rejoiced when those under him became greater than he was

Barnabas actively sought out Paul and wanted him as his ministry partner (Acts 11:25ff); he had neither jealousy nor fear of losing his

---

[6]https://en.wikipedia.org/wiki/RuthBrewerEisenberg. (Accessed October 23, 2017).

own position. Acts 12 first called their mission team "Barnabas and Paul;" one chapter later Acts uses the term "Paul and Barnabas." From this alone, we can conclude that Barnabas was able to promote people to such a degree that they became bigger than he was. Such a spiritual attitude can rightly be termed "the Barnabas principle."

It is rather common in the Bible for great men of God to share a ministry, e.g., Moses and Joshua, Elijah and Elisha, Paul and Barnabas. But what if one of them becomes more prominent than the other? What if the younger one is better, or just more popular? I believe that a crucial point in our ministry is to let others grow and increase under us, with us, and even ahead of us. That is the right Kingdom attitude. The opposite approach is to keep people small, to perceive them as a threat to one's own position. The vital question is: "Am I willing to allow others to grow into their full potential, even if that means that they become bigger than me?"

Such a question was once put to Elijah. It initially perplexed him to the point that he couldn't give a straightforward answer. "When they had crossed over, Elijah said to Elisha, 'Ask what I shall do for you before I am taken from you.' And Elisha said, 'Please, let a double portion of your spirit be upon me.' He said, 'You have asked a hard thing'" (2 Kings 2:9f). Elijah answered that Elisha was asking a hard thing, a difficult thing. What might he have meant by that? Three possibilities come to mind: (1) Elijah was so convinced about his own greatness that he doubted anybody could match him; (2) he thought little of Elisha, and therefore, found it hard to believe that he could fit his shoes; or (3) most commentators agree that "a hard thing" is something only God can accomplish.

Yet Elijah gave evidence that he had embraced that possibility by telling his younger colleague that God would grant his wish if Elisha witnessed Elijah's ascension. He was not too opinionated about himself, neither did he look down on Elisha. And it happened exactly as Elisha had hoped (if we can measure anointing in miracles). During his lifetime, Elijah worked 14 miracles, whereas Elisha performed double the number—28, the last one occurring after Elisha died (2 Kings 13:21). Mourners threw a dead man into Elisha's tomb, and when his body touched Elisha's bones, the man was resurrected by that touch.

I would say that the primary function of missionary ministry nowadays is to invest oneself in other people, to build them up, and then to hand responsibilities over to them. Consequently, a missionary should not become too absorbed by his own ministry, but rather his chief business is to promote the ministry of others. This can only happen with an attitude of servitude and humility. Bayless Conley writes, "The ministries of some of the greatest preachers died with them because they fell short in producing spiritual sons and daughters. Sure, they were excellent when speaking in front of large crowds. They were perhaps able to constantly fill the largest halls in their countries. But they were losers when it came to spiritual parenthood. And for that reason, their work only blossomed during their lifetime."[7]

Last, let's consider Jesus' earthly ministry. If there was ever a minister who did not need to see others greater than himself, it was Jesus. Yet (and this is truly mind-blowing), Jesus had the humility to extend the prospect of it. He did not talk about his character or personality, but about his works, announcing, "Truly, truly, I say to you, he who believes in me, the works that I do, he will do also; and greater works than these he will do because I go to the Father" (John 14:12). Now, I do not think that we should try to compete with Jesus' miracles. Nevertheless, the lesson we must learn is that, if the Son of God can have the humility to promote others to such a degree, then every one of us should be actively involved in advancing others as well.

Training People for Ministry and Missions

Aspects of the Training Element

Second, we need to train the senders as well as the goers. Earlier we discussed training the senders, and today we have different methods of going. Earlier we discussed training senders. Let us look now at the training aspect from the perspective of the goers. Today we have different methods of going. Traditionally, while many go for long-term service, we also have people who go for short term missions service.

---

[7]Bayless Conley, *The Miracle of Mentoring: A Biblical Guide to Spiritual Fathering* (Tulsa: Harrison House, 2001), n.p.

We need to understand, however, that although helpful in many ways, short-term service has its limits. For instance, you cannot adequately impact an unreached people group with short-term service. While it provides some assistance, we need people who are committed to spend years in building the foundation for the church, in translating Scriptures, and in holistically transforming the society.

Despite its limitations, short-term ministry can nonetheless be very beneficial. It offers both a taste of the mission field and a testing of one's calling. It also provides the possibility of valuable service, even for those who will never become long-term missionaries. Often, after their experience on the field, short-term workers have become good motivators for missions in their home church and have learned the importance of spiritual warfare. Also, in many cases, short-termers do become long-term missionaries.

The concept of "tentmaking" has long been a part of missionary work. Paul partly financed his missions work by being a professional tentmaker (Acts 18:3); and the successful Moravian missions movement used this principle 300 years ago. Tentmaking today has different nuances. Sometimes it means having a job in a foreign country while at the same time being a witness for Jesus Christ and, with other believers there, establishing a church or promoting the work of an existing church. Another form of tentmaking (or naming it as a separate category) is "Business as Mission." For example, an entrepreneur may start a company in another country with the intent of becoming a model of a Christian businessman displaying Biblical ethics and ready to serve as a witness for Jesus at every opportunity. Some who emphasize the influence of Christian values in the business world call it "Business as Transformation," believing that Christian ways of working will help transform society. Simply offering employment in an environment of unemployment makes a big difference and gives a good testimony for Christ.

Some missionary work requires special skills and training. For example, there are more than 2,000 languages still without the Bible. Missionaries who concentrate on Bible translation need special training as well as academic skills. Also, more and more, people use sports, art, and music to build genuine contacts with the people in other countries and cultures. Another special type of missions work is aviation, which requires professional pilots and aviation technicians.

Media, with all its various modes (especially social media), is an increasingly important way of spreading the Gospel and discipling converts. People who serve in media need to be professionals, since media organizations often have built their own "brand." They sometimes specialize in specific languages and areas in the world. The danger here is that media specialists may not cooperate with the churches and other mission organizations in the country where they operate. However, there are plenty of examples of fruitful cooperation between the media organizations, mission organizations, and churches.

One very interesting special missionary force deserves special mention. A team of former drug addicts and alcoholics from Russia, who are now believers and freed from their addictions, have gone as missionaries to many different countries in Asia, Europe, and to other parts of the world. They know where to find the drug addicts and how to properly approach and minister to them. Some years ago, Arto's colleague from Fida International, Rauno Mikkonen, and Arto visited their leaders. Together we established a cooperative training program, which they have continued and have learned different ways of doing missions.

General Principles in Spiritual Formation

Throughout the Bible, the overarching principle of spiritual formation is that preparation for the ministry happens through the relationship of father and son.[8] Abraham taught Isaac, who taught Jacob who, in turn, taught his sons. And those nomad chiefs had plenty to teach. In addition to imparting their knowledge about animals, plants, geography, weather, diplomacy, and trade, these fathers shared spiritual experiences with their children. Spiritual knowledge is a treasure to be handed down from generation to generation.

---

[8]Spiritual parenting includes mothers and daughters, of course.

If we fast forward hundreds of years, we find Israel's religion had become institutionalized under Moses. While almost everything changed, the principle of spiritual education remained the same. The Levites formed a clerical class of their own in which one could only receive training for the ministry if one's father was a Levite. Levites' active ministry only started at the age of 30, thus they had sufficient time to learn beforehand. Israel softened the principle somewhat during the era of Elijah and Elisha. There were a few schools for prophets, and admission was through charisma rather than genealogy. Yet those schools formed around a senior prophet, a charismatic fatherly figure, upholding the principal to a significant degree.

The main principle of ministerial formation seen in the New Testament was still spiritual education through fathers and mothers. So, how did Jesus learn? He did not enroll in a famous school of theology, although such schools existed during that time. Neither was our Lord a visitor to public places of learning, or to libraries such as the famous one in Alexandria. Rather, Jesus learned through the Scriptures and through the unbroken connection to his heavenly father. He gave direct reference to such learning processes (e.g., John 5:19).

By the first century, much had changed, from little secluded Nazareth to a church in an urban metropolis like Corinth. Yet, Peter, John, and Paul understood that they were teaching parents of their spiritual sons. Paul named three individuals as sons (Timothy, Titus and Onesimus) and that was a spiritual, not a biological, bond. Spiritual fathers educated candidates like Timothy and Titus by spending much time with them, travelling and ministering alongside each other. Mentors educated their spiritual sons in the Scriptures and instructed them in how to teach the Scriptures (2 Tim. 2: 2). Paul still cared for his spiritual sons once they started in ministries on their own. His pastoral letters give ample evidence of his support. The entire process was mentoring at its best, and it certainly produced tremendous results.

What might have been God's intention when designing spiritual formation to take place in families? One striking difference between teachers and parents is that the latter will not only add knowledge, but will also shape the character of their students. Although parents can be very warm-hearted and supportive, there also can be a lot of friction between parents and children. This always leads to character formation. The ideal of spiritual parenthood thus stands for holistic training of both mind and character. That is exactly the training future pastors and missionaries need. Any training system preparing missionaries that concentrates solely on academic qualifications, without taking attitude, character, and holiness into consideration is bound to fail. Local congregations and mission fields do not just need clever people, they also need good ones!

Now, given the fact that this principle is a Biblical stronghold, what are we to do with it nowadays? Let's translate "fatherly" into "pastoral." Were we to do so, one change would be the qualifications deemed necessary for serving as Bible school teachers. Almost everywhere, Bible schools choose lecturers because of their academic achievements. However, would it not be good to also appoint pastors to these schools? Instructors can be passionate about doctrine, but we need teachers who are passionate about their students. Teachers with a pastoral gifting do not see the contents of their subjects as the most important element in education, but rather the hearts and inner growth of their students. They see their foremost ministry not in the conveyance of knowledge, but in the edification of students. Consequently, they take an interest in their students and love spending time with them.

If it is not possible to go to the extent of having more pastors appointed as lecturers, then a Bible school would at least do better by appointing a counselor, campus pastor, or chaplain for the students. A school can be a very lonely place; and students sometimes have their minds filled with theology, but their hearts remain empty. Schools must check such an imbalance by actively appointing people to look after the students' inner well-being.

A mentoring system would support graduates' spiritual formation. Fatherly and motherly instructors can accompany an intern or vicar. Churches can partner with a school, and their pastors can be involved in mentoring students. The big question regarding each individual student is always: How and with whom is that person being involved in relationships? Nobody should go through a theological education system without having a mentor.

Teaching the Bible and Its Application

Perhaps the most important requirement in spiritual formation is to help students come to a comprehensive understanding of the Bible and teach them how to apply the Word of God in their ministry. When it comes to Bible knowledge, it's not so important for students to learn about every fork and knife in the tabernacle, but to acquire the big picture of God's plan of salvation. The narrative approach works well here, and hermeneutics is a key.

I (Ulf) advise every school I visit to start with a basic introduction in hermeneutics, rather than with heavy theological subjects like Christology or Pneumatology. Students, (especially in Europe) read the Bible through too many theological lenses—i.e., doctrines. It is best to leave those "lenses" aside at the beginning, so that students will later read doctrines through their own understanding of the Bible. They will have become theologically mature when a healthy hermeneutic has become their yardstick in any theological question.

My daughter Marja, in learning to be a chef, studied a lot about food ingredients and menus. But it didn't stop there. She also learned how to cook—at a stove and for people. The same applies to the Bible and Bible schools. Students need to learn how to apply the Scriptures in different settings. Are they able to interpret the Bible in a spiritual and creative way so that they can feed a congregation over the years? Are they able to lead someone to Christ by showing salvation from the Scriptures? Can they "rightly divide the Word of God" (2 Tim. 2:15) so that it will then become more understandable to their listeners? Can they use, and quote, the Scripture passages to defend major doctrines? Do they know the themes of the various books of the Bible so they can find the right antidote in them for problems they will encounter in church and mission situations? Are they able to edify themselves through prayer and the Word of God, especially when times get tough? These skills are major, and any Bible school that does not teach these things is not worth its name.

Contextual Theology to Balance Local and Global Elements

There is not one Bible school in the world that teaches an undiluted doctrine. Our teaching is always an interpretation of the Bible, and our culture also conditions our interpretation. Our denominational direction, plus our personal preferences and spiritual passions further impact our interpretation of Scripture. Moreover, nowadays we can group the two major influences into "local" and "global" elements.

The Local Theology Element

Jesus is a good example of a local theologian. His entire teaching and preaching ministry made use of the culture around him. He drew inspiration from family life, work life, plants, animals, customs, sayings, the weather, historical events, etc. He actively built those culture-related elements into his teaching to illustrate his message vividly. It is also intriguing that Jesus made use only of Jewish culture. Granted, he could have explained Greek vocabulary, impressed his audience with examples from far away countries, or quoted strange books to his listeners. Yet he stuck to his own Jewish cultural roots so that his teaching was understandable and applicable to his listeners.

The local theology that Jesus practiced had three dimensions. *First*, it consisted of local contents. Someone once said that people are always interested to learn more about something they already know, and Jesus made good use of that principle. He consistently started with an example familiar, and oftentimes self-explanatory, to the people—e.g., "Nor do people put new wine into old wineskins. . . ." (Matt. 9:17), and "Now suppose one of you fathers is asked by his son for a fish; he will not give him a snake instead of a fish, will he?" (Luke 11:11). Then, Jesus built spiritual truths into those everyday examples. Everything he said made sense to his listeners on a practical level, whereas the spiritual dimension remained hidden to many.

Second, his theology had a local perspective. For example, I (Ulf) started researching and writing African church history under a professor at the University of Malawi. In a draft of one of my early books, I wrote how a European missionary prepared himself to go to

Africa, then described his farewell service in his home church, ending with "And he went to Africa." My professor did not accept that sentence. He blotted it out with red ink and corrected it to read, "And he came to Africa." Now, going or coming may not seem to be much different; but in this case, it was a question of perspective. I was in Africa, and so I had to learn to see everything from an African perspective. That is why it was important to say the missionary "came here" rather than "went there." In 2015, I was serving as a consultant with a church in Russia to set up their own School of Missions. As we were planning the subjects, I suggested the following subheading to the subject of Church History: "From Jerusalem to Vladivostok," which the leaders enthusiastically accepted. Moreover, the students could immediately understand that the subject was to draw their attention of major historical developments right to their own church. A local perspective is something that many churches throughout the world are craving for. They want to build and develop their own identity, and local theology is the way to do it.

Third, local theology consists of local learning and teaching methods. Sometimes Jesus taught in short, concise sentences, a method his listeners grasped from the book of Proverbs. He also knew how to tell a story that would keep his audiences spellbound. I once met a boy who was dyslectic. Letters were just one big jumble to him, so he had serious difficulties with reading and writing. He was much better with numbers and anything that was visual, such as pictures which he easily understood. Unfortunately, his parents did not enroll their son in any local school, but rather home-schooled him via computer. There, the poor fellow sat in front of the screen many hours a day trying to read and type. That teaching method did not at all match his faculties. One key question is always whether a culture tends more to narrative, literal, or visual aspects. After this, the governing question should then be: Which learning method holds the greatest promise to root the contents in the students' minds?

The Global Theology Element

Having just explained local theology in a nutshell, let us now focus on global theology. It primarily consists of traditional notions and doctrines that have found worldwide acceptance. Take, for example, the doctrine of the Trinity. The concept that there are three distinct persons in the Godhead is something about which Roman Catholic, Protestant and Pentecostal Christians largely agree. The same can be said about the human and the divine nature of Christ. Again, most churches teach this, including all evangelical and Pentecostal denominations. Also, while the New Testament does not spell out Trinitarian and Christological doctrines in detail in the New Testament, yet we have broad and global consensus about their veracity. Such traditional doctrines constitute one part of global theology.

Another aspect of global theology is non-traditional, and concerns more the mode of spiritual education. Teachings and even entire curricula have now reached worldwide distribution. Theological Education by Extension (TEE) or Global University come to mind. I know schools in Nepal, Kenya, the USA, and Cambodia that share the same study guides and textbooks. Although the courses were not written in those countries, they have been translated into the local languages. Moreover, the mass media have literally spread international elements in theology around the world. People upload and watch sermons, and digital books are readily available to anyone with an internet connection. Furthermore, most missionaries are proponents of international theology. They come from faraway places and they usually import theology. A few movers-and-shakers have driven Charismatic Christianity, and their teachings are also everywhere through various communication methods.

Contextual Theology as the Needed Balance

Local and global theologies need not be antagonists, nor do we need to give value to one at the expense of the other. The task is rather to balance the two. The formula that Taiwanese theologian Shoki Coe developed reads: "local theology + global theology = contextual theology.[9]" Therefore, no one needs to start from scratch and invent

---

[9]https://en.wikipedia.org/wiki/Contextual_theology. (Accessed October 27, 2017).

their entire theology anew. Many people have worked before us, and the church does have a rich heritage to draw from. Thus, internationally available materials have supported spiritual formation.

What is currently in greater need, in my estimation, is an emphasis on local theology. We have too much international theology, and suffer from a lack of local theologians and their work. Pastors may not address many issues in congregations because the answers to them are not in the textbooks of global theologies. To all Bible school teachers, I offer the following: It is always better to write one's own subject (if possible) than to translate another's work. The last word, and best perspective in this matter, belong to the local churches. Do the teaching contents benefit the local church? Do the graduates of the Bible school benefit the local church? The more local a training program can be, the more acceptance a school will have from local congregations.

Theory and Practice

Nowadays, the rallying cry seems to be, "Spiritual training must be practical." Bible schools advertise their programs as being "practically orientated." A lot of such phraseology is futile, for training initially needs to be theoretical. Any practice, skill, action, or operation is based on theoretical knowledge. We call any action carried out without theoretical support an "affect" (when people act in the heat of the moment), and affects usually lead to accidents. Very practical professionals, such as carpenters, plumbers, and even potters, base their skills on theoretical knowledge and they teach it to their apprentices as well. In the same vein, how could anyone ever underestimate theoretical preparation for the complex qualifications of a pastor or missionary? The problem is not theory, but the application of theory. It's the interface of theory and practice that decides whether a teaching program is feasible or not. Thus, the question always is, "What kind of theory will make it 'out there?'"

Some students just can't wait to get out of the classroom and into a pulpit. While otherwise an understandable motivation, it's obligatory to us as their teachers and leaders to give them a wider perspective. While students, they have the chance to devote most of their time to studying and acquiring a scriptural foundation for their ministry. They will probably never again enjoy such an opportune time as this, and they will miss it sooner than later.

I cannot go into detail in this chapter so will only mention one more major ingredient that theological education should entail, and it has to do with "practice." Given the fact that our graduates will be working with people for the rest of their lives, it's important that they acquire people skills. Many Bible schools neglect this. A successful graduate should not only be skilled with the Bible, but also have social competence. Traditional curricula often offer a limited number of social subjects. A course in counseling is perhaps the most common in this cluster and much needed. Some schools have introductions to psychology and sociology. Communication is also a fitting skill in this cluster. Pastoral theology should be about people. Nowadays, the subject of leadership is widespread, and rightly so. Of course, Bible school training alone cannot impart all that's needed in people skills. Thus, perhaps it's an area where one will learn more outside the classroom than inside. Yet, emphasis matters, and so any school that creates space for these subjects in its program will do well.

Specific Principles Related to Training for Missions

All the above-mentioned principles apply for the training of missionaries as well as pastors. Although these principles are the most important, let us turn our attention to those that apply specifically to mission's work.

Attitude and Character Development

We will only win this world for Christ when Christians are ready to leave their comfort zones. A missionary is, by definition, a person who has left one group of people behind to reach out to another group of people. To that end, missionaries give up their jobs, the comfort and coziness of family, and forfeit a budding career (including a pastorate) and bring their children to strange places and potentially expose them to the dangers of disease, crime, terrorism, etc.

The best mission schools that I know are currently in east Asia. They place significant emphasis on prayer, and teach their students to be servants to people and hard workers for Christ. It's all about attitude. Although a school cannot create the commitment that missionaries must find by themselves before the Lord, it can provide a framework or an atmosphere whereby such a commitment is easier to make. The truth is, that upon arrival on the field, missionaries become children again. If a church is already there, they may welcome them as great men or women of God. But the fact is, that what missionaries hear, smell, and feel comes closer to the perception of an infant; they must re-learn most aspects of life in that new environment. It takes humility to become such a child, yet it is the approach our Lord chose for himself.

The Bible as Cross-Cultural Common Denominator and Tool

Having already talked about the Bible under "General Principles" above, it can also be said that the Bible is the "number one ice-breaker" in multiple mission settings. For example, a missionary is to speak in front of a church in his target culture (a rather common occurrence). He will have a better chance of winning his listeners over, to both the message and himself, if he shares a simple Gospel message in an interesting way that edifies the church. The Bible functions as the common ground, and its skillful application can be a bond between missionary and listeners. They will understand, and remember that the missionary was able to communicate the word of God to them. That way, we somehow already regarded him as "one of us."

Yet the opposite is also true (and has happened many times). A missionary may speak in a way that's too complicated, too aloof, or too abstract, thus losing the moment of bonding between him and his target group. One common mistake that missionaries tend to make in such a situation is that they try to explain themselves, their ministry, and the need for it. Yet the prime importance in such a setting is to serve people spiritually, not to explain everything about oneself. The hearers will accept a missions approach only after they have accepted its bearer. I have heard compliments about other missionaries from local people who said, in essence, "He came as a brother." That's a wonderful way to put it—and to follow.

Teaching and Promoting Cross-Cultural Skills

Missionary candidates are preparing to live and work in a different culture, and that requires skills and character. Students must learn to see themselves in the context of the other culture. The best subject to promote this awareness is a thorough introduction to Cultural Anthropology. The spiritual foundation and veracity for this comes from both Christ's incarnation and the initial cross-cultural spread of the Gospel in Acts, which the Holy Spirit so powerfully implemented.

Schools should expose students who are monolingual to foreign language learning during their training. No matter what language one must tackle, there are some principles of acquisition that the school should teach. We should teach students to learn a language, not just study it. The difference is that, with the former approach, they will come to speak it.

Students with a multi-cultural background have "stolen a march" on those whose background is less complex. Yet, a lot of informal cultural cross-pollination goes on at Bible schools; and should encourage this diversity should. Ways to support this include cultural festivals, "strange recipe days," learning songs in a foreign language, a national dress show, etc.

Experience and Professionalism

It's important that a missions training program have some experienced missionaries teaching at least some of it. Although not necessary for every subject, many students gain tremendously when there's "a voice from the field." I further recommend that the schools expose students to a wide variety of missionary ministries—e.g., evangelists, church planters, Bible teachers, Bible translators, agricultural experts, and Christian development workers. Schools should also give Missionary kids (MKs) expression. Further, they should address the specific role of the spouse in the field, single missionaries, and so on. Also, missions schools should have special functions that deal with issues like missionary marriage, tropical sickness prevention, homesick children, etc.

Partnering in Missions

More than ever before, mission ministries are connected and interdependent. Mature missions agencies do not start their own church in a foreign country, as if Christianity without them is still at day one. Rather they look to partner with already-existing churches (local or national). Such partnerships often result in win-win situations and, in certain contexts, are a must. For example, it's doubtful that a white Western missionary can effectively reach a hostile and/or isolated jungle society in Indonesia. I know that this has happened; and while it might make for good and adventurous missions reading, such cases are the exceptions that prove the rule. Yet, that same white Western missionary can enter into a partnership with an existing church in Indonesia to raise that church's awareness of the unreached jungle people. Then, the missionary can help train and support the local Christians to go there.

I think that charismatic and Pentecostal believers are especially prone to neglect the principle of partnership in missions. We are oftentimes vision-driven and tend to see no obstacles as we exercise our faith in God's promises. A strong sense of calling should not lead to a lone-wolf syndrome. The lonesome missionary hero working alone has no Biblical role model. Rather, missionaries in the New Testament were team players without exception; and wherever they went, they first tried to contact those local people who were already in touch with God—be they Jews or so-called "God-fearers" (i.e., those from a pagan background yet interested in the God of Israel).

Missions usually organize partnerships on a bigger scale. Denominations from different countries work together, and mission directors plot together, to see that mission strategies from different organizations intersect at a place or ethnic group. Yet (and this is my plea), let us sensitize students and teach them about partnership in missions during the training.

A Holistic Emphasis

Nowadays, anything but a holistic approach is a hard sell. People in poorer countries need answers to their most pressing problems, those in animistic cultures seek relief from fear, and many in Western civilization are looking for meaning from an otherwise shallow philosophy of life. People want to know how to live. Spirituality is one aspect of life, but not the only one. Thus, educators should acquaint students (at least theoretically) to the fact that, "out there," people need more than a sermon. Bible schools are an excellent resource tool, and they are also a networking agency between missionaries, churches, and ministries. Additionally, more and more countries will never grant a visa to the "professional missionary." We need professionals with secular skills; through this avenue, professionals may come to minister spiritually, too. While the scale tips toward spirituality for mission organizations, Christian development agencies usually focus on the material and educational well-being of people. So, for those working in a development cooperation, holistic means not to neglect the spiritual aspect of human beings.[10]

Training in Making the Case for One's Ministry

Usually, missionaries are simultaneously busy in production and advertisement, and many need to learn how to communicate effectively to the home base. Missionary candidates will also be wise to be open to criticism when it comes to their performance in front of a home church. Do people understand what you are trying to get across? How can you break down an oftentimes complex ministry situation into understandable segments? We must constantly relearn communication because of three factors. First, the situation in the field changes, and the missionary's communication must change accordingly; second, communication methods change rapidly, and the missionary needs to keep up with those changes; and third, the missionary's support base changes over the years. Not only may new supporters be hard to find, but winning them through the old methods and channels of communication is almost impossible.

Some missionaries excel in preparing their periodic newsletters, while others are poor at it. Also, some ministries are an easier sell (e.g.,

---

[10]Robert Odén, *For Better for Worse: The Role of Religion in Development Cooperation,* (Bromma, Sweden: Swedish Mission Council, 2016).

serving poor children compared to an outreach to Muslim minorities). Diverse ministries call for tailor-made approaches when trying to garner support. Missionaries must learn all this, and schools would do well to show how to address the communication task in practical ways.

Modes of Training for Missions

Worldwide, there are different modes of missions training. Some training takes place only in local churches. I know of one small mission organization where most of the training prior to sending missionaries happens in the organization's office. However, if we order missions training according to levels of intensity, and focus on what is happening in Bible schools and colleges, the following modes emerge.

Missions Awareness

Some churches continually emphasize missions, beginning in Sunday School for the children, all the way up to Bible and coffee gatherings for the elderly, where people speak about missions, pray, and collect money for the cause. Most countries have missions conferences, which focus on raising missions awareness, and missions motivation. These mission conferences do not train people for the job of a missionary. Churches and Bible schools have sermons and teach short courses about missions. One of the most successful tools in this regard has been the Kairos Course, which I recommend for every church to employ.

Short-Term Training and Field Experience

A good number of Bible schools provide short-term courses that include missiological basics for a few weeks followed by field experience, which can last up to half a year. Various other Bible schools offer specific courses on missions, with perhaps a total of twenty hours of instruction in their three- or four-year curricula. This is modest if there happens to be students in class who want to make missions their lifelong ministry.

Missiology as a Discipline in the Curriculum

Other schools teach missiology with multiple courses devoted to the subject; the initial one is "Introduction to Missions." Subsequent ones might include: "Mission in the Old Testament," "*Missio Dei*," "Paul's Ministry," "Theology of Missions," "History of Missions," and "Mission Strategies." Schools might address issues like "Calling," and such common subjects as "Evangelism and Church Planting." A serious missiology curriculum will likely offer "Cultural Anthropology" as well as specialized approaches, such as "Witnessing to Hindus," "Witnessing to Muslims," "Ministry in Urban Areas, and/or Tribal Missions." Some books of the Bible make excellent mission textbooks (e.g., Jonah and Acts). The studies of "Apologetics" and "Comparative Religions" are also important courses. We give more ideas in the first chart.

Chart 1

POSSIBLE DISCIPLINES AND SUBJECTS FOR A MISSION SCHOOL CURRICULUM			
Foundational Missiology	**Applied Missiology**	**Practical Courses**	**Specialized Courses**
Missiology incl. Missio Dei	Cultural Anthropology, incl. Worldviews	Kairos Course (with its emphasis on UPG)	Islam
History of Missions	Evangelism	Team building	Hinduism
World Religions	Church Planting	Rehabilitation Ministry	other religions...
Hermeneutics for mission contexts	Mission Strategies and Methods	Foreign language courses	Ministry to children & youth
Kairos Course (for overview and motivation for missions)	Linguistics – introduction to languages and language acquisition. Also preparation for Bible translation ministry.	Courses in combination with development studies: agriculture, construction, human rights, gender issues, empowerment, political justice etc.	Regional specialization: e.g. Pacific Islanders, urban ministries, "tribal" missions and so on
Missiological hermeneutics on particular Bible books: Jonah, Acts and others	Personal & family life of missionaries	Media and communication techniques	Mission among cults & sects
	Cross-cultural communication	Support-building and fund-raising	Bible translation
	Prayer life and spiritual warfare	Leading / pastoring in foreign contexts	Outreach to handicapped people
		First aid and medical intro	Practical courses in electrics, plumbing etc.
			Humanitarian aid
			Preparatory courses for tentmakers and Business as Missions
			Internet, Social Media
			Radio & TV

The Mission Line

Some Bible schools offer a main direction of studies (which is similar to a major in the United States) in which the students may graduate. Some Bible schools have pastoral, leadership, deaconship or mission lines. A mission line means that students will graduate with a certificate, diploma, or degree in missions.

The Mission School

A missions school's entire purpose is to concentrate on missions. This is becoming common in countries where the ordinary Bible school serves the homebound candidates. Many mission candidates are looking for a training institute devoted solely to missions. Many mission lines and mission schools offer vocational or academic degrees to their students.

The second chart shows a curriculum for one such mission school in Papua New Guinea. Significantly, the church has decided that mission candidates must complete their Bible school training before entering the mission school. This allows he mission school to have a more focused and shorter curriculum.

Chart 2

CURRICULUM FOR A SCHOOL OF MISSIONS IN PAPUA NEW GUINEA		
Foundations	Missions	Skills
The Kairos Course	Evangelism & Church Planting	Cross-cultural Communication
Theology of Missions	Apologetics for Melanesia	Spiritual Parenthood
Melanesian Worldview	History and Strategies of Missions	Practical – tentmaking - instructions
Missionary Life	Spiritual Warfare and Accompanying Signs	
	Ethnologies of Oceania	

Sending and Partnering

Sending-Related Considerations

First, we must answer these questions: By whom are the missionaries sent? What is the role of the local church in sending missionaries? What is the role of the national missions department or organization? Who is involved in the sending decisions? Who is screening the candidates? Who has the responsibility for financial support? Who defines the principles of employment?

It is common for new senders to experience failure in the sending process. Initially, things look fine. The missionaries are motivated, the senders enthusiastic, and the first reports from the field inspiring. But then the situation can change dramatically, communication falters, financial support lags, and (often sooner than later) the missionaries return from the field. Sadly, this scenario can paralyze missions work for years.

So, what went wrong in the sending process? Dr. Peter W. Brierley made a study of the reasons for new senders' failures. At the top of his list were these: lack of home support, lack of a call, inadequate commitment, disagreement with the sending agency, and problems with peers.[11] When we look at those symptoms, we can divide them into structural deficiencies and inadequate screening. In these circumstances the structure does not sufficiently protect and support the missionaries (i.e., human resource management is poor), and because of inadequate screening, the structure sends people without a genuine calling and/or incomplete training. We must rectify the above weaknesses, so that both the missionaries and their sending bodies can avoid many disappointments.

A crucial issue also is where we should send a missionary. Can the Holy Spirit speak to this, as was the case with Paul and his team? What kind of principles does the missions department or organization follow? How much do the senders honour Paul's policy of "preaching

---

[11]Peter W. Brierley, "Missionary Attrition: The ReMAP Research Report", ed. Taylor, *Too Valuable To Lose* (Pasadena: William Carey Library, 1997), 94.

Jesus where he is not yet known?" Until now, the centre of gravity of missionary work has not adequately moved toward unreached people groups, thousands of whom still have not been adequately touched. Of course, this question of focus is not purely black and white. Mobilizing new senders is an important part of contemporary missions work. The World Assemblies of God Fellowship includes 368,000 churches.[12] Because so many of them are in the non-Western world (where thousands of churches have not yet sent any missionaries), we see a tremendous seedbed for new missionaries. However, that requires cooperation whereby experienced senders can help newer senders by sharing their experiences of failures and successes.

In Indonesia, one Pentecostal Bible school has specialized in world missions. While the national church of the school's denomination is still formulating its missions structure, the Bible school has already worked for decades in sending missionaries to unreached people groups. Over the last ten years, for instance, it has trained and sent out sixty-three pioneer missionaries to work among eleven unreached people groups. One missionary died a martyr, but most of the others are still ministering to people who have not yet heard of Jesus Christ.

Partnering-Related Considerations

Many decades ago, when missionaries arrived on their fields, they were pioneers as no missionaries had ever been there. Today, you will hardly find a country in the world without Pentecostals, evangelicals, and other Christians. Of course, you will also find many unreached people groups amongst whom nobody is working. However, if believers are already there, would it not be wise to contact them and find out what plans might they already have in place to reach that group? Are they ready to work together for winning the lost?

New senders would benefit from global and continental networks. Two such global networks are the Pentecostal World Fellowship (PWF) and, as already mentioned, the World Assemblies of God Fellowship (WAGF). A loose network known as "Empowered 21"

---

[12]WAGF (World Assemblies of God Fellowship) Connection magazine, September 2017.

connects all Pentecostal Charismatic Christians. What is the benefit of these networks? Almost all countries of the world have a Pentecostal presence. So, if you want to send a missionary to country X, you can contact these existing network organizations to learn who the key persons in that country are. Through them, you can establish a dialogue to map the possibilities of your missionary to work in that context.

Choosing the partner with whom to work is an important decision, for it is not easy to know the proper partner who is interested in building a relationship. Many pastors and churches in poorer countries often think they will get some material benefit from that relationship. Thus, it is much safer to build contacts through trustworthy channels than just start with the first interested contact. The above global and continental networks represent expertise, have clearly articulated doctrinal statements, and provide a common spiritual foundation. Their leaders meet annually, which builds a personal network. In other words, you know with whom you are working.

New Senders' Potential Needs

Adequate Screening

The fact that too many missionaries sent by newly sending countries soon return home indicates problems regarding candidate screening. The best place for assessing new candidates is their home churches. Thus, we need to equip the leadership of those churches to understand the basic requirements of missionary work. In addition, we need to test the candidates in their service at home before sending them out.

The senior pastor of one Finnish pioneer missionary asked him to win 200 souls before going out, which he did. Over time, that missionary became a key figure in the development of an African Pentecostal denomination; today, about one million people attend its churches' Sunday morning services.

Adequate Training

Too many new missionaries are sent without proper training (in fact, some with no training at all). The principal of a mission school in Brazil related to me that many pastors and mission candidates have told him that they do not see the importance of missions training, either because there's too little time before Jesus returns, or because it's too expensive and there are better ways to use the money. However, it's this principal's experience that eighty percent of missionaries who go untrained return home within two years.

Strategic Thinking

Sometimes the missionaries (and their senders) are not familiar with the missions map, so they only go where missionaries have traditionally gone or where their friends are. Because of this lack in strategic thinking, only a marginal number of missionaries are working among the unreached people groups, of which there are still almost 7,000. Another oft-neglected segment in missionary work is children. Most decisions to follow Jesus are made between ages 4 and 14, which is known as the "4/14 Window." To really impact the next generation and build continuation for our work, we cannot disregard, or minimize, the importance of reaching children.

In several cases, the focus of fruitful missions work can still be in countries with already established churches. However, some strategic resources in these are weak. Thus, expertise in Bible education, media work, children's ministry, student ministry, "Business as Mission," or world missions training may be needed.

Proper Structure

Plain enthusiasm is not enough. People can be inspired, but long-term results are likely insignificant if we do not provide the proper structure. The sending structure may be in place, but the training may be poor, or the partnering structure missing. Even mobilization can be weak if it is based only on inspiration without a firm theological conviction and commitment. An African proverb says, "If you want to go fast, go alone; if you want to go far, go together." Building a proper structure takes time; but having that structure, you can go far.

Appropriate Partners

One Asian country, eager to start missionary work, found partners in Africa. After some time, the Asian leaders realized things were not in balance with the partner, so they cut off the connection. According to their culture, that meant losing face, and the leaders felt ashamed. The result was that the denomination's world missions program ceased for a long period of time. Fortunately, later they launched a new, more balanced approach. The benefit of Pentecostal and other evangelical networks is that you have trustworthy leaders who are connected to each other, and those networks cover almost the entire world. When the statements of faith are similar and the values and principles easy to share, then cooperation will be based on solid ground.

Experienced Mentors

Another benefit of networks is the contact available with others who are involved in world missions. Through those connections, new missionaries can find mentors. In 1991, we started a Pentecostal mission network which today is called the Pentecostal European Mission (PEM). Soon after, we encouraged new senders planning to start missionary work to join us. We also invited experienced missions leaders and missionaries from other member organizations to help teach and train newer missionaries. All this allowed new senders to learn from experienced senders at our annual meeting and other gatherings. Further, they learn from each other when sharing their difficulties and successes. The same experience takes place in networks on other continents.

Realistic and Meaningful Evaluation

We can learn much from our victories and difficulties. However, some people minimize the opportunity to so via a process of evaluation, or even forget to use evaluation. Every missions organization or department and missionary needs a system for recording and assessing their activities and the results. When Jesus sent the twelve, and later the seventy-two, out to evangelize, he gathered them together after their return. Although they were excited about the results, he brought reality to their evaluation to ensure they kept the correct focus on their work. They should not be afraid of Satan but they should avoid his trap of becoming proud. Jesus reminded them that they should concentrate on grace and that their names were written in the heavenly book (Luke 10:20).

Experienced Senders' Potential Needs

Interest in Others' Programs

Every missions sending unit needs supporting churches or people behind it, which is why they must keep their supporters informed and satisfied. Aware of this, Paul, with his team, reported inspiring news and shared the challenges they were facing. There is the danger, however, when a person's own success becomes so important that they forget the main goal. Missions and missionaries are there to serve and build strong partnerships with the national church and other missions. Thus, they are driven in the same way as Paul—Christ preached everywhere he is not yet known.

In extreme cases, the projects of the sending unit can become so important that they are not at all synchronized with the goals of the receivers. Missions should never be money-driven or self-focused but rather Spirit- and partnership-driven. The Spirit always leads towards unity because that is the nature of the Triune God. Therefore, open dialogue between sender and receiver is a must. If dialogue is lacking, missions will do things inconsistent with the priorities of the receivers. While these "things" might be good ideas, they are probably not effective in meeting the more important needs. For instance, building some houses may inspire the people at home, but the national church might be lacking support for Bible education. In the context of developing a missions structure for a national church, we do not recommend exporting the model of the sender. Instead, communicating with the structure of the missions organization is much more fruitful. Many elements may function in a foreign setting, but senders can easily miss some cultural aspects and fail to properly analyze them; thus, we do not realize the best results.

Partnering from an Equal Base

Genuine partnering takes place between people who are on the same level. Feelings of cultural superiority (many times hidden) can spoil otherwise good possibilities. This can be very challenging if one partner has more resources than the other, because money starts to lead. So how can we avoid this? You really need to see your partner as an equal; and that can only take place from a spiritual perspective. You need to see yourself as a sinner redeemed by the blood of Jesus, which is also, true for your partner. It is there that you are on the same level. You can try whatever else, but you will soon find that you feel differently on some matters and that partner's views are not fitting with your pattern of life.

We can, and must, learn to understand the partner's culture, and this is usually a long process. The starting point might be an ethnocentric attitude where we judge the other culture inferior and our own as superior. If we have the willingness to understand the other, the journey toward healthy inter-ethnic relations can begin. This can then lead to integration with the other culture. We may reach the summit when the differences in cultures are involved as leveraging factors.[13] In the best scenario, the Western-structured way of working can become enriched by the Asian sensitivity to relationships, by the warmth of the African family atmosphere, etc. In which way can these things influence the building of a missions structure?

Holistic Understanding of the National Work

Westerners often enter other cultures bringing their own cultural patterns with them, not really understanding the context into which they have come. Sometimes they assume proclamation as the only

---

[13]Arto Hämäläinen, 2005, 150.

solution to meeting the population's needs. However, if the people are burdened by sickness or social problems, their ability to concentrate on the message will be hindered. Non-Western people often have a better holistic understanding about life even though they have limited resources to help. Thus, it is wise for new missionaries to listen and learn so that, together with the local people, they find the way forward. It is not usually a case of one method versus another, but the goal is to find a balanced way of combining views of living in this world while having eternity in view.

Spirit-Driven Projects Rather than Money-Driven Projects

Missions work needs money, but money should not direct missions. One day, a missionary from a rich Western country arrived in a poor country claiming to have millions of dollars. Asking the local church leaders if they would be interested in starting a social project with that money, there was, of course, no lack of interest. However, the result was money-driven projects instead of holistic help provided for the people. Money was the dictator, not the Holy Spirit.

Teklu was a young student when a British missionary led him to Jesus. This missionary did not have much money or great projects, but he did see a young man in his spiritual need. Upon returning home, the missionary thought he had not accomplished great things. Decades later, Teklu met the missionary in the United Kingdom and told him how the Holy Spirit had led him. He had served as general secretary of a large Pentecostal church in his country, and later as director of a mission that concentrated on unreached people groups. Over the years, thousands of people had found the Lord as Saviour. Hearing this, the old missionary broke into tears, because his going had not been in vain.

A "360-Degree" Understanding of Missions

In New Testament times, the receivers became givers and senders. In our time, too many churches stop moving forward when they have reached stability. Receiving churches become satisfied with fifty to one-hundred members, they look inward, and lose evangelistic or missional zeal. Sadly, the same takes place in their mission target.

When local churches become "established," they often feel they have reached the goal, but that is not true. The churches will not reach the goal before the receiving church has become a sending church. The church needs to come full circle, praying that God will send workers into his harvest, and then sending the people whom the Lord is calling into service.

United Attitude

Western culture is becoming more and more individualistic. It's me, my ego, my interest, my privilege, my benefit. That same virus is poisoning believers as well. It's not that we shouldn't ever think of ourselves, but Jesus taught us to the love our neighbour as ourselves. When we miss "the other," we lose balance and fall. The danger of individualism is not only a threat for believers, but also a risk for local churches. They, too, can become individualistic, taking interest only in their own matters. The New Testament churches were not independent; they were interdependent. Ego-centered individuals and ego-centered churches lose their ability to see the needs around them. Jesus said, "Open your eyes and look at the fields" (John 4:35). He saw people harassed and helpless and had compassion on them (Matt. 9:36).

Receiving Partners' Needs

Cultural Sensitivity

The central subject in missionary training is how to meet a foreign culture. The receiving (target) culture is not necessarily any better in meeting the new missionaries, especially if they have had no previous experience in doing so. Their normal reaction is to reflect on the situation from the point of view of their own culture. Thus, we need a bicultural journey.[14] This includes some stress for both sides, but that kind of bridge is important for proper understanding and fruitful cooperation. A wise receiver dares to take this journey by trying to

---

[14]Paul G. Hiebert, *Anthropological Insights for Missionaries* (Grand Rapids: Baker Book House, 1985), 235-236.

understand the missionary who is coming from another culture. At the same time, there is no other alternative for the person coming to serve the church or group of believers in a new culture.

Ethno-Relative Approaches

Rosinski contends that we deal with cultural differences in one of two ways—either ethno-centric or ethno-relative.[15] In the former, we tend to ignore differences or evaluate them negatively, or at least minimize their importance. That kind of attitude leads to separation, isolation, denigrating others, feelings of superiority, or trivializing the differences. It is very sad when the relationship between missionaries and their receivers is characterized by ethno-centrism. On the other hand, a positive development in cultural relations includes recognizing and accepting differences, and adapting to them—even integrating and leveraging the divergences. All these positive attitudes are what Rosinki calls ethno-relative approaches.[16] At the highest level, differences generate concepts for something new; they lift the situation up to the next level. This leveraging means, for example, that the Asian relational culture connecting to the Western way of logical planning creates a benefit for each.

Guiding Missionaries Coming from Another Culture

Sometimes the arrival of a new missionary does not generate much attention among the receiver. The reason may be poor communication from the sender. However, it can also be the consequence of a weak receiving structure. Perhaps the structure has appointed no one from the receiver side to be a contact person and mentor for the new missionary. The lack of support can also happen because a poor relationship between the sending mission and the receiving national church exists. In a best-case scenario, the national church has a designated person to serve as a mentor for the newcomer. It also includes communication by which the sending mission has prepared

---

[15]Arto Hämäläinen, 2005, 150.
[16]Ibid.

the receiving church for the arrival, has appointed a mentor for the missionary and with a job description.

A National Strategy

It is much easier for new missionaries to find their place if the receiving national church has a strategy. Unfortunately, that is not always the case. Sometimes the communication is only oral, with different leaders likely emphasizing different things. Although strategy does not require a written document, it certainly is much easier to communicate strategy that's in a written form. This is very helpful for people coming from the outside, because they can know national work's serious concerns and what the goals are. It also helps the sending mission understand what kind of missionaries are needed and whether those interested in going have the right capabilities to fill the need.

Knowledge or Expectations of the Missionary's Gifts and Skills

If the country has a long history of receiving missionaries, the models from the past will likely dominate their image of a new missionary. The receiving country may have esteemed the pioneer missionaries, which easily leads to expectations of the same skills, gifts, and characteristics of the next generation of missionaries. This is true, although the context of today is apt to be totally different. For this reason, a sincere analysis of the current situation is needed so that the expectations will be more realistic and fitting for the actual needs.

Questions for Reflection

Are members in my church feeling that they are a part of the mission force? How are the members in my church trained for missions as senders and goers? What kind of sending structure is available for the churches and missionaries in my context? With whom is the mission organization in my context partnering in the receiving country? What are the pitfalls in our mission context?

Chapter 3

Designing the National Missions Structure

Designers of missions structures must give thought to the different levels of structure in the initial stages of designing a national missions structure. We need to ask include the following questions: What is the structure on the local church level? What is it on the regional level? How should we design the national structure referencing the other levels? What kind of power is to be given to the different levels? What kinds of decisions are to be made, and at what level are they to be made?

Designers have one major decision to be made: whether there should be a missions department of the national church, or a totally separate missions organization. Also, we can look at this issue from either a theological or a pragmatic point of view. From the theological view, if we agree that missions are the reason for the existence of the Church, then it's natural to place the missions structure at the core of the church. In that way, we easily legitimize a missions department, for we keep world missions in the heart of the church and not outsourced to any other entity.

The pragmatic approach to this matter, however, unveils a different reality. Some church leaders do not understand the missional character of the Church, and thus are hesitant about, or even antagonistic toward, the idea of a missions department. The undeniable fact is that pastors are in a key position for world missions; and if they are not promoting a missionary vision, it's very difficult to move on.

In one European country (that had been a part of the communist world after WWII), some interest in world missions arose at the turn of the 21st century. I was invited several times to teach a small group of interested pastors who wanted training. Besides myself, others from the USA and Sweden also came to teach. Some pastors in the group were eager to start a mission's department in the national church, but the national leaders were not interested. However, these missions-minded pastors did not give up. After many years and many unsuccessful attempts, they concluded that another route had to be taken, and that path was to establish a separate missions organization. Wisely, they did not make that decision in a spirit of opposition but by negotiating with the national leaders, who eventually agreed to allow establishment of the missions organization. Over time that missions organization has proven to be a real blessing for both the churches and for global missions. Today it is an integral part of the national denomination, and it has already trained and sent out about 70 missionaries in a little bit more than one decade's time.

Unity is a divine principle, of which the Triune God is the ultimate example. Thus, whatever type of missions structure is developed, this divine principle should be honoured. Regardless of the structural model selected, promotion of unity among the national leaders and local churches should be sought.

Missions Structure Should be Culturally Relevant

When the Protestants started establishing missions organizations more than 200 years ago, they followed the idea of voluntary association, with the churches unofficially involved in the process. "Sodalities" (voluntary associations) instead of "modalities" (the churches) took the active role.[1] Later, however, the churches awakened to the missions vision and began forming their missions departments, organizations, or societies. One important milestone impacting that

---

[1] Ralph D. Winter, "The Two Structures of God's Redemptive Mission", eds. Ralph D. Winter and Steven C. Hawthorne, *Perspectives on the World Christian Movement* (Pasadena: William Carey Library, 1999), 220-230.

development was William Carey (*An Inquiry into Obligation of Christians to Use Means for the Conversion of the Heathens*) in 1792. These entities reflected the culture of the Western countries. It would prove to be a mistake to bring such structures into a non-Western church without contextualization.

The structure of the national church affects missions structure. Three main categories of church government—congregational, Presbyterian, and episcopal—are found throughout the world. The Pentecostal movement, which started more than 100 years ago, was understandably influenced by these categories, because many who experienced the Spirit baptism were a part of those churches. As a result, we have all three types of Pentecostal churches, along with some mixtures. For instance, the Nordic Pentecostals have a congregational-Presbyterian model. When the Pentecostals established churches on the mission field, they often replicated the model of their sending country. There are exceptions, however, as some African, Asian, and Latin American leaders have been able to adapt features from their own cultures into their church structures.

The Western world has developed a more individualistic culture, which has brought challenges to cooperation with other cultures in some activities. World missions efforts need the collaboration that we saw in the New Testament. Many non-Western cultures are collective by nature. Their cultures, which require working together, provide good starting points for missions.

Cultures also differ in their understanding of "power-distance." In many Western democratic countries, the power distance is small. For example, if you have something on your mind, you can approach your boss without it causing problems. In most non-western nations, however, you cannot approach the boss, or higher leader, without a mediator. The distance is too great for an ordinary person to breach. Those two differences affect missions structure as well. Of course, every cultural aspect must also be evaluated from a Biblical perspective. Differences were also present at the time of the primitive church, which is why Paul (who was a Jew) wrote the Corinthians (who lived in the Greek culture) that they only understood him in part. He was hoping that their cultural understanding would increase so he could be fully understood (2 Cor. 1:14).

Cultural clashes are always a danger in missionary work, which is why missionaries must be well-trained in cross-cultural understanding. Behaving in a mono-cultural way in a cross-cultural context is always seed for misunderstanding and conflict. Understanding a foreign culture is a long journey and one full of surprises. Learning begins with sensitive listening. It benefits both individuals if, as a result, they understand the strong and weak points in their own culture and in the other culture. The most difficult to analyse is one's own culture; and you cannot do that without a "looking-glass." What is that looking-glass? It's the other culture. Only by learning that other culture can you fully grasp the strengths and weaknesses of your own.

When a missionary forms a national church, there needs to be an understanding of that nation's culture to structure a culturally appropriate missions department/organization there. A proper understanding will avoid replicating unsuitable elements of the missionary's home culture, and a good analysis of the host culture will help prevent undesirable features from infiltrating the mission structure.

Chadwick Mohan, one of the pastors of New Life Assemblies of God Church in Madras, India, has researched the effect of Western influence on South Asian church leadership and identified both positive and negative influences. Key among the negative factors were: secularism, capitalism, and consumerism.[2] Mohan emphasizes a selective approach towards Western influence. The church leadership in Asia must wisely discern, taking the good and leaving the not-so-good.[3] He is concerned particularly about the weakening of spiritual and moral values in the Western world. We Westerners have much to learn from the South Asian church context.[4]

---

[2]Chadwick Mohan, *Towards a Conceptual Framework for Church Leadership Formation in Urban South Asia* (Chennai: New Life AG Church, 2009), 239.
[3]Ibid., 237.
[4]Ibid., 262-263.

The Structure Should Foster World Missions

The missions structure must protect and foster a missionary vision. In what way is the structure promoting world missions at the national and the local church levels? Is the structure promoting international connections for the national church? Are all four strategic areas of missions (i.e., motivating, training, sending, and partnering) well covered?

The missions structure should provide protection from power misuse and corruption, which is important for sustaining positive results. The fostering aspect will not function if such protection is not in place. There needs to be safeguards against a dictatorship style of leadership, which is a particularly great danger in a strong power-distance culture. One such safeguard is that every leader must be responsible to someone. Paul gave us a good example of that by reporting on his ministry among the Gentiles to the apostles in Jerusalem (Gal. 2:1-10). It's also good to note that the Holy Spirit was behind that ministry initiative, for Paul went to the Gentiles because of a revelation (Gal. 2:2). Thus, his reporting was not prompted by any human bureaucracy but by a divine principle—i.e., showing responsibility to God-appointed leaders. Structured leadership protects missions from the misuse of power!

Additionally, the structure has to protect each missionary. That is why a leadership structure must be clearly built in the sending unit as well as the receiving unit. Missionaries are in a challenging position as they serve both the sending structure and the receiving structure. To really provide a proper covering, these structures must be in legal harmony with national laws. In its best form, structure will hinder misbehavior as well as pave the way for problem solving.

Too rigid a structure will hinder flexibility, which is needed in complicated life situations. In turn, too loose a structure will not provide protection against failure. Typical weak points of structures include a lack of delegation, poor empowerment, and unclear roles. Also, too many leaders tend to concentrate all the power in their own hands, which prevents them from releasing any power and function to capable persons around them. Jethro recognized this problem in Moses' leadership (Exod. 18:17-23). Seeing the work was too heavy for

Moses alone, Jethro recommended that Moses select capable men to share the burden. Likewise, Paul advised Timothy to entrust responsibility to reliable men who were qualified to teach others (2 Tim. 2:2).

Spiritual leaders' major responsibility is to empower their followers. Paul described how God has provided apostles. prophets, evangelists, pastors, and teachers "to prepare God's people for works of service" (Eph. 4:11-12). Church leaders are to be coaches and trainers for believers in the use of ministry gifts for practical service.

In hierarchical cultures, everyone must know, and keep, their particular position in the whole cultural structure (including family, working context, church and all other social involvements) and not aim higher or lower than their rank. In egalitarian cultures, people are freer to strive for a higher position, which allows many to dream of starting low and then climbing to a higher role. An egalitarian culture offers space for that, whereas other cultures are more rigid. Individuals in a hierarchical culture need to understand the position(s) for which they have been born. The roles tend to be predictable—for instance, if your father is a pastor then your role also will be that of pastor. While this may be God's plan, the danger is that the assumption is only a cultural expectation. Thus, the leadership of the Holy Spirit is decisive and very important. Discernment is needed in order to know what is the true will of God is, versus what is only a cultural expectation.

The missionaries' understanding of their roles is important. For what purpose have they come? Does the sending missions organization have the same understanding of missionaries' roles as the receiving national church? If not, both missionaries and receivers will experience disappointment, needs will not be met, and dreams will not be fulfilled.

In order to overcome disappointments, the involved parties need to be ready to evaluate the situation. If both parties do a proper assessment, then the work can be developed. The learning process continually helps to improve quality. Evaluation often leads to changes, small and great; but many people only want stability, not change. Our creator God has not ceased his activity. Jesus said that his Father works all the time, and Paul encouraged us to be transformed by the renewal of our mind (Rom. 12:2). God is for change, transformation, and renewal. If the people in our organizations forget this, we are on our way to stagnation, decline, and eventual demise.

Questions for Reflection

What cultural aspects are involved in building a missions structure? In what ways are the church and missionaries protected by the mission structure? In what ways is the mission structure in my context fostering missionary work?

Chapter 4

Missions Structure

There are three main types of missions structures—the networking model, the cooperation model, and the hierarchical model. Below, we define each one and discuss its strengths and weaknesses, and we also point out in which countries or cultural contexts it is practiced. Following that are a few suggestions on how you can strengthen your missions structure.

The Networking Model

In this model, churches and the national missions organization/department are loosely yoked in their world missions pursuits. Although networked, these entities generally have few or no binding documents or agreements; they simply want to be in relationship with others to benefit from each other's missions experiences. In some instances, their connection on an official level is simply to receive recognition from the authorities (such as government or organizations which grant legal permissions) in other cases, the network is stronger and more organized. But typically, these entities are quite independent of each other. Thus, usually they have no common strategy, although they may follow some agreed-upon basic guidelines. However, there's a strong tendency towards democracy in these networks; and when they make decisions, it is with the support of all participating units.

When it comes to world missions, this model has several strengths. Those strengths include: the possibility for each entity's growth; the benefit from learning about, and adopting, the best practices of others; and the potential for conducting some joint activities.

The weakness of this model is "disintegration." It can never enable effective, larger-scale joint activities that require a solid structure and strategy for implementation. Some examples of joint activities include ministering to unreached people groups; running Bible and/or missions training institutions; carrying out Bible translation projects, large evangelistic campaigns, mass media efforts, or large social projects; and providing humanitarian assistance in catastrophic situations. These efforts are usually too much for one, or only a few, entities. Also, it is difficult for them to develop sufficient expertise to meet the massive needs.

Swedish, Norwegian, Danish, Icelandic, and Brazilian Pentecostals commonly use the networking model. However, they may also use certain variations.

The Cooperation Model

In this model, the local churches and the missions organization/department of the national church form an official cooperating unit. Thus, the cooperating entities must define the roles of both counterparts: They must designate the responsibilities of the local churches, and those of the mission department/organization. Usually they have a constitution that spells out the roles of each entity and outlines the decision-making process. A common strategy helps everyone to understand why, for what, and how, the work is done. Also, a manual of operations helps in management. This strategy saves time because they do not need to define the mode of operation for each situation individually. The commonly agreed upon, and clearly stated principles, help in coming to conclusions and finding solutions.

The benefit of this model is that the local churches and the missions department/organization can concentrate on their natural strengths. The churches, as a basic unit, can motivate people and give fundamental training for missions. They can also take financial responsibility and provide spiritual support. Whatever their roles are in the details, they are strongly involved in implementing the Great Commission.

The weakness of this model becomes apparent when either entity loses its vision; this always affects the whole system. If the churches are not active, they do not assist in the efforts of the organization, which results in the organization lacking the necessary personnel and financial resources. If the organization becomes weak, the churches will struggle to send people and find partners in the target country. Another weakness is that, in case they do not clearly define roles, their decision-making becomes slow and ineffective at best. With nobody making the decisions, the local sending church, the missionary, and/or the partnering national church become frustrated. Therefore, roles and responsibilities need careful consideration.

Pentecostal churches often use the cooperation model, although the roles in various countries differ. The Assemblies of God USA follows this model, as do many European Pentecostals.

The Hierarchical Model

Many cultures characteristically employ "pyramid thinking;" their people often experience top-down leadership. The top leaders thus have a great responsibility; but that does not mean that they are leading alone as a dictator. They may have a leadership team helping and advising them. They may also be responsible to an executive committee or similar entity. In missionary work, this model means that there is a missions director. Some Pentecostals have built a global hierarchical structure, while others have a national structure. But in every case, the top leaders direct the system.

In this structure, the local churches' missionary efforts are under the leadership of the national missions department/organization. On the field, the missionaries are responsible to the regional or country leaders. Many times, the national structure includes the local, regional, and national levels so that leaders, along with their committees, are responsible at all these levels.

The benefit of the hierarchical model is that usually the responsibilities and decision-making power are clear, and fit well with the thinking of each counterpart (if their culture is also hierarchical). This model can also offer opportunities for mission activities on all levels, since it covers all levels; also, its constitution and manual of operations can give clarity to daily work. At its best, this model is effective and culturally relevant. While the more democratically oriented cultures might consider this model strange, it's powerful if it encourages input from all levels of the hierarchical structure, or involves everyone in implementing missions-related decisions.

One weakness of this model is the potential for the misuse of power. Leaders will likely be effective if they promote valuable activity. However, they can become dangerous if they lose the vision but love the power. Another weakness of the hierarchal model is the danger of quenching creative initiatives from the grass-roots level. Remember, the Holy Spirit can speak to any "Ananias" to go. Is there space for that in this model?

Many Asian, African, and Latin American cultures reflect the hierarchal model. Their national church structures tend to use hierarchical thinking; therefore, it is natural to find their missions structures following the same principle.

Strengthening Your Missions Structure

Be Open to Evaluating and Possibly Changing Your Model

As we have seen, all three models have their pluses and minuses. Thus, evaluation is important to identify and eliminate any negative developments. Assessors should follow spiritual principles, and focus questions on the main goals. Among those questions might be these: Is the structure helping us to reach the unreached? Is the structure satisfying the motivation of the local churches for world missions? Is the structure supporting the work of the missionaries? Is the structure offering a good basis for partnership with the receiving churches or the cooperating partner organizations?

The Finnish Pentecostal missionary work has gone through major changes. Initially, it practiced the old missions agency model (in this model, the churches' role was weak; they only gave money and supplied people for the mission agency, which then was responsible for all activities). Then, it moved on to the networking model, giving the responsibility of missionary work to the local churches. Last, it adopted the cooperation model, which has developed and is becoming increasingly effective.

Seek to Learn from Others

New senders often can get much help from each other. While they can, of course, learn many things from experienced senders, their practical questions are likely to differ from the questions of the those senders. Thus, it is natural for them to identify more closely with the experiences of those who are dealing with the same challenges. The forums where they meet with their new sender colleagues are helpful to them. The consultations of the Pentecostal European Mission (PEM), Pentecostal Asia Mission (PAM), Africa Pentecostal Mission Fellowship (APMC), the Latin American Pentecostal Network, and others, all provide a chance for such encounters.

In the current world situation the largest number of Christians are in the South (or, the "gravity" of Christianity is in the South), so we speak in terms of South-South relations. The churches in South America, Africa, and Asia benefit especially from their mutual cooperation in world missions. Of course, the North also needs forums connecting the new senders. For instance, the national leader of Bulgaria expressed how helpful Romania's experience as a new sender was to Bulgaria as it took its first steps as a new sending country.

Questions for Reflection

Which model of the three presently best fits my cultural context? What can we learn from others in developing a structure? What kind of weaknesses, or threats, are likely in our mission structure?

Chapter 5

Key People on the National Missions Team

The components of a national church's missions department (or independent missions organizations/ agencies) usually consist of a mission's director, a mission's board, various specific-function committees, a missionary training director, and a field structure that includes regional directors or coordinators. This chapter will describe each component's responsibilities and the issues it addresses, plus the desired qualifications for people who serve in those positions to ensure the department's/organization's success.

Missions Director

Vision is the decisive factor for growth and success; and missions directors (or executive directors, directors of missions, general secretaries, or other title designating the leadership role) is key to articulating that vision and directing its implementation. However, they need not (or should not) carry the load alone; for they can delegate, empower others, and develop work assignments to facilitate implementation. Visionary leaders are prayer-oriented and are prepared to make important decisions. Jesus gave us a model for this by always praying before big decisions (e.g., choosing the disciples, his prayer battle in Gethsemane).

A common way of describing the two main aspects of directing are the terms "leadership" and "management."[1] The leadership role addresses the question of "what," and the management role address the question of "how," both of which are needed. As the top leader, the missions director should be capable of answering the "what" question, which entails vision sharing and vision keeping, while others can respond to the "how" question.

Identifying Desired Qualifications

What are the things that qualify one to serve in the role of missions director? Following are what we feel are the qualifications that should be at the top of the list. Missions directors should:

- *Have a calling from God to carry out the missions vision.* God should recommend them, just as God recommended Paul and Barnabas in Antioch.
- *Have at least some experience in world missions.* Often, such people have served as missionaries; however, they may have gained experience in other ways, such as demonstrating a consistent and intensive interest in world missions and a desire to hear the life stories of missionaries. These qualities may compensate, to some degree, for their potential lack of missionary experience. Nobody is fully qualified; thus, everyone likely has some strengths evident, while they still probably need to develop some areas.
- *Have an understanding of local church work.* The role of local churches in world missions is crucial, thus they need to understand the dynamics of the local church, especially in regards to missions.
- *Are cross-culturally oriented.* Sensitivity towards other cultures is a key matter in these leaders' work. Gaining that sensitivity to other cultures is a life-long journey that calls for commitment.

---

[1] Arto Hämäläinen, 2005, 98.

- *Are people-oriented.* Missions is about people, not about money (although, of course, missions needs money and we must manage it well) or about projects (although they're included in the whole picture). But missions priority concern is for people and their welfare. Again, Jesus gave us examples. He was not only interested in the disciples' effective ministry, but he also cared about their physical well-being, such as when he removed them to a remote place to rest.
- *Are "team players."* Paul illustrated this quality. He was not a loner, but surrounded himself with co-workers (both Jews and Gentiles). As their leader, Paul shared his vision with them and created a "we" atmosphere (Acts 16:10). Sadly, today we see leaders who only dictate their orders and do not seek, or accept, input from co-workers.
- *Are led by the word of God.* Their decisions are always theologically grounded.

Recognizing Leadership Styles

In electing leaders, it's critical to analyse the abilities of the candidates for the position. One important measure is how the style of their leadership is characterized. Janet Hagberg placed styles of leadership into the following six categories.[2]

Powerlessness (Leading by Force)

This type leads by fiat and force, thus inspiring fear. These leaders are insecure and lack authentic power. They utilize force to get people to follow them. History provides many examples of how dictators engendered fear through their oppressive systems. Unfortunately, some spiritual leaders have perpetuated this.

---

[2]Ibid., 100-101.

Power by Association (Leading by Seduction and Created Dependency)

These leaders rely on their supervisors and do not take risks by making their own decisions. They have never developed their own competencies, which makes for leadership characterized by dependency and seduction. Perhaps this is the reason why Paul, sensing the danger of Timothy becoming too dependent on him, reminded Timothy that "God has not given us the spirit of timidity, but a spirit of power, of love, and of self-discipline" (2 Tim 1:7).

Power by Controlling (Leading by Symbols)

Power is a controlling affair for these leaders, who are often ambitious, competitive, charismatic, and egocentric. Although via their personal powers of persuasion they might otherwise inspire a "winning attitude," it's the bane of having to control that keeps them from moving forward to the next stage. These kinds of leaders might otherwise do great things, especially in a culture where the leadership structure is pyramidal. But their compulsion to control is too strong. This style especially hinders the empowerment of younger leaders.

Power by Reflection (Modeling Integrity and Inspiring Hope)

Leaders of this nature use influence to express their power. They are known for being strong, reflective, competent, and skilled at mentoring, thus these leaders model integrity and inspire hope. This style of leadership is fitting for pastoral leadership. Paul, in writing about the Thessalonian believers, expressed how they became a model for others (1 Thess. 1:7). The reason they were good examples is that they imitated Paul and the Lord (1 Thess. 1:6). At its best, our ministries can inspire others to follow our model.

Power by Purpose (Empowering to Spur Love and Service)

These types of leaders are known for their vision and are sometimes called "the irregulars." They are not ego oriented; they are ready to give away their power and let others lead. They are self-accepting, calm, humble, confident of life's purpose, and spiritual. Their hallmark is empowerment that inspires love and service.

Notice how Paul motivated the Macedonians to give generously although they were poor (2 Cor. 8:1-5). The secret was that he had proclaimed the grace of God in Jesus so clearly, and with such enthusiasm, that the Macedonians were ready to give even their bodies to serve God. The decisive factors were the experience and understanding of God's grace that spurred their purpose.

Power by Gestalt (Imparting the Wisdom That Creates Inner Peace)

The expression of this style is wisdom. These leaders are comfortable with paradox, unafraid of death, quiet in service, and ethical. Their power is almost invisible; thus, they inspire inner peace in those around them. The best example of this kind of leadership is Jesus. His very presence solved many problems; even children, intuiting the peace around him, wanted to come close to him. In summation, the question is whether leadership is a natural trait, or can people learn it? At a certain level, God gives leadership ability to the individual person.

As believers, we need to also remember that the Holy Spirit empowers us. Thus, people who seem to be very shy can become leaders through a supernatural anointing by the Spirit. However, those who have natural talents likewise need the Spirit's empowerment to avoid the temptation of trusting in their intrinsic abilities.

Missions Board and Committees

Usually, there is a missions board that makes the biggest decisions. Who should be on that board and what qualifications should they have? Of course, boards need members with experience or expertise in some form. If the missions organization is relatively new, it may not be easy to find people with significant and long-term experience. In that case, vision and attitude are the decisive qualification factors. Later, it becomes easier to find people who have missionary experience on the field.

The board needs the perspective of missionaries, but the input of the churches is needed as well, in order to reach a good balance between the different valuable elements. At the outset, the board members are likely to be pastors or key people involved in the sending aspect. Also, lay people such as church elders who have experience in leadership and management can be valuable, provided they are proven spiritual leaders.

If the national church in the sending country includes regional levels, then the missions structure should reflect that in its makeup. Otherwise, implementation of the missions program can become weak in some location in which it serves. However, the roles of the national, regional, and local levels should be made abundantly clear to avoid unnecessary duplication and delays in decision-making.

Missions organizations can have different committees to help with various aspects of the process; but one must be careful in establishing new committees. Too heavy a structure can paralyze the work. Every committee or task force should meet a clear and definite need. The organization should also evaluate how long different committees, or working groups, need to exist. It is better to establish them for a certain purpose with a clear goal.

Director of Missions Training

Training missionaries is one of the key activities of a missions organization. Here, a close relationship with various missions training entities is very useful. Collaboration with the Bible schools and theological institutions will help in developing a program that meets both the theological and missiological needs. If, for some reason, such cooperation is not possible, then the missions organization needs to develop its own training program. Whatever the arrangement, a missions organization needs a key person for directing missionary training. At the same time, it is important to remember missions also need training for short-term and special ministries, as well as the thorough equipping of senders. It's the responsibility of the director of missions training to address the need for the whole spectrum of missions education. Directors of missions should have a good missiological understanding. Also, they need personal experience in missions connected to talents in the educational arena. Missions candidates must have the ability to balance academic and practical goals. Many times, knowledge of spiritual warfare is much more important for them than all the theories of missions.

Field Structure

Who is making the decisions in the country of the missionary's calling? Is it the sending missions organization, or the receiving national church, or the missionary? Many tensions and problems have arisen when the field structure has not been clear in this matter. In the past, missions organizations played the central role, and the missionaries had to ask the home country what to do. Over time, the "three-self principle" helped much in moving decision-making from the sending country to the field. London, New York, Berlin, etc. should not dictate what to do; it's the national/local church that must decide. Churches in the field need to be self-governing.[3]

The role of the missionaries becomes a challenge in this process. Should they only obey what the national church is prescribing? What about the missionaries' role if the missions agency suggests or implements something? Where is the voice of the sending church? Such questions are usually solved by creating a "field structure" for the missions organization. While different variations are possible, nevertheless, someone must represent the missions organization so that the receiving national church can hear its voice. The missions organization represents the sending church. If each local church tries to have its own dialogue with the national church, the situation can become chaotic. However, when the missions agency represents the local church, the national church has a clear counterpart.

The sending country's missions organization needs a face in the foreign country. Such a face is represented by people called "regional directors" (if they are responsible for a larger area) or "field

---

[3] American, Rufus Anderson and British, Henry Venn developed the three-self principle in the 19th century, and later a fourth principle, self-theologizing, was added. The three-self principle was central also in the writings of Roland Allen. In the Pentecostal missiology Melvin Hodges, the Assemblies of God missionary in Latin America, developed this as a central principle of AG missions which has been practiced as well by many other Pentecostals, as well as in many other evangelical missions.

coordinators" (if the responsibility is for one country alone). This does not mean that regional directors or field coordinators would decide on behalf of the national church, for ownership should belong to the national body. But they can officially represent the sending missions organization and give a face and voice to it. In some cases, there is also a committee consisting of some missionaries that helps the regional or field directors/representatives.

The field structure will be unstable if the national church is not developing a counterpart to the missions organization. With whom should one discuss missions-related issues? Is the national contact person always the same person, or is it a different person depending on the matter at hand (e.g., church planting, Bible school, humanitarian assistance, development work, special ministries)? So, structure is a common concern of both the sender and the receiver. In building that structure, the builders need to design the problem-solving process and clearly spell it out. If both counterparts know what process is in place before a crisis occurs, that can save much time and energy; and most importantly, finding a solution comes easier. Good field coordinators, or regional directors, should be cooperative and respected by the local missionaries. They have a learning mind-set, are open to the ideas of others, are encouraging and help their co-workers find their talents. Working in a cross-cultural context requires a sensitive, flexible mindset with much patience.

Questions for Reflection

What qualities would best suit a mission director in our context? What is the role of the possible mission committees in our leadership structure? At which levels are committees needed? Who has the responsibility for missions training in our context? How will we build our field structure?

Chapter 6

Decision Making

Decision-making can be difficult, and a measure of that difficulty may stem from culture-related factors. In those cultures where communication tends to be indirect, the decisions dealing with problems connected to people might be very sensitive; and decision makers need to find a way to communicate properly while avoiding "loss of face." In cultures where communication tends to be more direct, people might have to slow down and allow more time for the decision-making process. The key is showing respect for each culture by involving the right people to help in the situation. Finding a mediator is often a good solution.

Another cultural factor in decision-making deals with uncertainty avoidance. In some cultures, uncertainty avoidance is weak, while in others it is strong. If it is weak, one can be ready to take risks; if it is strong, one avoids risk. In missionary work, we cannot avoid risks. Jesus took a huge risk by choosing twelve ordinary men to spread his message to all the world. The church in Antioch, likewise, took a risk by sending Paul and Barnabas to unknown cities and countries to make Jesus known. So, we cannot avoid risks if we want to win the world. Because an individual's culture can influence decision-making, some are hesitant to move forward, whereas others are happy to take bold steps. In

---

[1] Arto Hämäläinen, 2005, 161.

either case, we need the leadership of the Holy Spirit to balance our actions. For some leaders, it means more time for consideration; for others, it means more boldness to move forward in faith.

In decision-making, besides cultural factors there are also structural factors to consider. Thus, it is wise to determine which "level" is best to make a decision. In hierarchical cultures, almost all decisions emanate from the top level, which places an enormous burden on the leader. Consider Moses' situation before his father-in-law, Jethro, advised him regarding delegation. The point here is not to overlook the experience and knowledge of elders, which many cultures appreciate. Western culture, however, often turns the focus on young people with their creative ideas, sometimes at the cost of neglecting history and experience. Would Malachi's prophecy about God turning the hearts of the fathers to their children and the hearts of the children to their fathers (Mal. 4:6) characterize our leadership? There is blessing when the older and younger generations are together; the problem is often that elders fail to invite younger people to participate in the decision-making process.

I (Arto) am thankful that, at 26 years of age, I was invited to serve as a church elder. In that position, I learned so much from the more aged brothers, such as their approach to difficult matters, attitude in talking about problems in a church member's life, sensitivity in dealing with failures of some, trustworthiness in counseling, wisdom in complicated problems, and prophetic vision in planning future activity. Serving with them proved to be a valuable forum for empowering and equipping my ministry. My hope is that every church and missions structure would involve the younger generation in decision-making, first as students and then, as authorized participants.

Responsibilities and Roles

Clearly defined, and agreed upon, responsibilities and roles within the missions structure will prevent many problems. Too often, people assume what others need to do, but no one has informed those "others" what they're to do. In this area, Paul was an example of good leadership. In reading his letters, we find clear instructions to Timothy, Titus, and many others. Yet he honoured their own abilities by not going into too much detail, which might otherwise have quenched their own initiatives. For instance, he said to Titus, "Do everything you can to help Zenas the lawyer and Apollos on their way and see that they have everything they need" (Tit. 3:13). He did not list different items or ways of helping but rather just instructed, "Do everything you can." It was up to Titus to find out exactly what he could do.

On the other hand, Paul gave precise role descriptions regarding church structure, which he practiced everywhere. The churches were to have elders, deacons, and helpers; and he clearly spelled out the requirements for elders and deacons. We can enact the same principles in our missions structures by setting down the responsibilities and roles in writing. Written agreements provide the opportunity to check on what everyone has agreed to. In Finland, when a new missionary goes to the field, the missions organization, the local sending church and the missionary all sign an agreement . If an agreement is only oral, mere memory can easily result in different interpretations, which could negatively impact an otherwise amiable working atmosphere.

Delegation

Moses had the responsibility of leading God's people—about a million of them—out of Egypt, then through the desert and into the Promised Land. That was indeed an extraordinary leadership challenge—and a tiring one. To help ease the burden, his father-in-law instructed him to delegate power; Moses would judge only the most difficult cases. By following Jethro's counsel, not only was Moses relieved, but all were satisfied (Exod. 18).

Many churches and missions leaders concentrate too much power in themselves. One result is that many otherwise capable people around them are sometimes frustrated by the lack of opportunity to learn by taking on new responsibilities. Paul, on the other hand, was always eager to delegate authority, which we see when he sent out Timothy, Titus, Tychicus, or others. The key point is that they did not go simply on their own, but as representatives of Paul. Experienced, respected leaders should recommend new workers and the younger generation for opportunities.

I (Arto) personally would never have been elected to several international responsibilities if many respected brothers in Finland and other countries had not paved the way. God used them to open doors for me. I had not been aiming at the positions to which I was elected; those positions had been prepared by the Lord, who uses people to make things happen. As stated previously, God needs Barnabases!

Empowerment

Empowering is different than delegating. Of course, we need the empowerment of the Holy Spirit, but we can also become an empowering force by him to others. Paul tells the Ephesians that God has given apostles, prophets, evangelists, pastors, and teachers to prepare God's people for works of service (Eph. 4:11-12). Leaders should empower believers for such service. We as human beings cannot empower others by trusting our human talents, but God can use us as instruments for it empowered by the anointing of the Holy Spirit. His gifts enable us to serve people in a way that equips them to serve.

The secular world also talks about empowerment. Research, however, shows that people cannot directly empower others;[2] but what they can provide is an environment of freedom and trust from which empowerment can be exercised.[3] This is also true for missions leadership, as Paul's ministry routinely confirmed. In emphasizing that Christ has set us free (Gal. 5:1), Paul trusted in his co-workers, many of whom he identified in his letters. He delegated duties to them and empowered them for various kinds of service. In that way, he was continually educating a new generation for missionary work and the expansion of Christianity. Every spiritual leader should be sensitive to the possibilities to do likewise.

One practical example of empowerment involved my first employment, which was in music education, before I (Arto) began church work and theological studies. Finland has one of the best educators for symphony orchestra conductors, Professor Jorma

---

[2]Bruce Beairsto and Pekka Ruohotie, "Empowering Professionals as Lifelong Learners," in *Professional learning and leadership,* eds B. Beairsto, M. Klein and P. Ruohotie (Tampere, Finland: University of Tampere, 2003), 122.
    [3]Ibid., 124.

Panula. A number of his students have become famous, now conducting some of the best orchestras in the world. So, what has been Panula's secret? He does not make them copies of himself, for they are all different in their styles and personalities. Instead, in his training he creates an environment in which their skills have space to sprout and blossom. Thus, they become creative in their own styles and personalities, not clones of Panula. We need the same in the Church—an atmosphere in which the Holy Spirit can ignite the gifts God has placed in us. We should be striving to create that in others.

Questions for Reflection

What are the biggest challenges for decision-making in our context? Are the roles and responsibilities clear in our missions structure? Do we practice delegation? If not, why not? Do we empower people in our missions structure? What are the positive factors promoting empowerment?

Chapter 7

Financing Missions Component Parts

In this chapter, we consider the funding needs of the three key components of missions work: the missionary, the sending missions department/organization/agency (i.e., entity), and the receiving churches—and the various sources from which funding support should (or could come). Also, we briefly discuss two other missions-related expenses: the missionaries' training and the education of their children. Also, we examine how we should (or could) meet these needs.

Financing Missionaries' Needs

Over the years, three main types (or models) of financial support have been identified. Following is a brief description of each.

- Model 1. Called the faith-missions principle, missionaries are not promised fixed salaries, but rather support is entirely dependent on the donations that come in to the missions entity from churches and individuals. (By and large, church-based missions have preferred that the money come from the local churches.)
- Model 2. The missions entity collects the funds and takes the responsibility to pay the missionaries' salaries. The local churches or individuals only send

money to the missions entity once the salary level has been determined. (The donors have no other practical role than to send in the money and, of course, to give prayer support.)

- Model 3. The local churches have the responsibility of supporting the missionaries. Some may work independently, while others work in cooperation with the missions entity. Unlike a missions department, or a missions organization, the supporting church decides the salary level and other financial responsibilities.

Whatever the financial support system may be, we must consider not only the missionaries' monthly salaries but also the kinds of travel expenses that sending churches or missions organizations will cover, such as mission conferences, regional gatherings of missionaries or other important events. Further, guidelines for work expenses are important. Also, supporters must agree on a policy for the working terms and holidays of the missionaries and how often they are to be paid when visiting the sending country.

Financing the Needs of the Sending Missions Entity

It is important to remember that the missions entity itself needs financial support. Thus, a portion (e.g., 5%-10%) of the local churches' offerings need to go for this expense. In some countries, the churches provide a certain sum per member for that purpose; in other cases, business profits from such products as books and DVDs have been used. In other words, there are a number of creative ways to find solutions. Unfortunately, some individuals are reluctant to give money for administration, but no activity can be properly managed without it. In one situation, a person offered to make a sizable donation for a certain mission field provided that none of it be used for administration. The missions director to whom the offer was made replied that perhaps it would be better if the donor himself delivered the money to that mission field.

Many people do not realize that every step of the missions-funding process has a cost. In the sending country, people are needed to receive, record, and bank-deposit the funds. In the receiving country, people must confirm the money's arrival and do the bookkeeping involved; still others are needed to make any designated purchases and/or forward those purchases or funds to the appropriate parties. Every step has its cost.

Financing the Needs of Receiving Churches

This issue brings us to the question raised by the three- or four-self-indigenous-church concept, a key principle of which is self-support. The initiators of this concept, Henry Venn and Rufus Anderson, argue that any needed financial resources should come from their own country, not from the sending missions entities.[1] The reason is that outside support leads to dependency, which, in turn, tends to quench local initiative. While application of this principle has usually borne good fruit, be aware that catastrophic situations could occur whereby humanitarian assistance would be the right way to respond.

Related to the above is the issue of support of the native workers. Although it would seem good to help support people who know the language and culture and who can work for a much lower salary than the missionaries, nevertheless, the realities are that we can quickly create dependency. Also, discontinuing such support is not all that simple. Further, we see that churches which are growing are also self-supporting. Again, there might be reasons in a few cases to provide support for a limited time, provided a system is in place for the decrease of outside support and the increase of local support.

Financing Other Missions-Related Issues (What and By Whom)

Training Missionaries

This question inevitably arises in regards to missionary training: Who should be responsible for, or at least involved in, the funding of any required training course(s)? Is it the primary sending church *or* the missions department/organization/agency *or* the candidates

---

[1]Craig Ott and J. D. Payne, *Missionary Methods – Research, Reflections, and Realities* (Pasadena: William Carey Library, 2013), 160-161.

themselves? Also, are there other sources to assist in the expenses involved in this training?

Educating Missionary Kids (MKs)

As with the above, who is responsible for that effort (and to what degree)? Should it be the parents *or* the sending church *or* the missions entity? In practice, this is often a significant burden for the parents; in some cases, this challenge has closed the door to missionary service. In some countries, the schools are very expensive; oft-times, the cheaper alternatives offer such a low level of education as to seriously endanger the children's future.

In Finland, decades ago, our missions department realized that this issue had become an obstacle to a family proceeding to the mission field. Our solution was that we would divide the burden of the MKs' education between the local churches, with each church paying a school fee per member. In that way, together they carry the burden of the missionary families. The missions entity coordinates this effort and carries the overall responsibility.

Member Care of Missionaries

Pastoring and counseling for missionaries has become more and more important in missions, and that needs the attention of the mission organizations/departments. Too many workers have been lost because of the lack of a proper pastoring/counseling/mentoring system. Many missions entities have created a system of people trained in pastoring or counseling who have abilities to take care of missionaries facing problems in their lives or ministries. Those activities, that at their best, prevent the unexpected return of missionaries from their working country, or, at the least, minimize the hurts of missionaries in worst cases need some financial resources as well. People in member care must be trained for their special ministry, and they need money for the emerging trips to help in needy situations.

Questions for Reflection

What is the plan and system of organization for missionary salaries? How are we covering the costs of the mission's entity? What are we doing regarding the costs of training missionaries and their children's education? Who is responsible and in what ways? What is the basis of motivation for giving to missions? What is the role of faith in giving to missions? How are we communicating the role of faith in missions giving being?

Chapter 8

Conclusion

The first step in starting a missions' program is to determine the leading of the Holy Spirit. He is the one who empowers people both to send and to go. Without people, the missions' structure is an empty shell, like the ruins of an old city without inhabitants. As at the first Pentecost, the Church can receive power through the Holy Spirit to become witnesses to all nations and people groups.

Just as in the New Testament, mission activities need goals: where to go and what results are desired. Setting appropriate goals is the strategy which simply determines success in fulfilling Jesus Christ's command to go into all the world and preach the good news about him. However, the strategy is an empty promise without a structure that offers a channel for implementation. The missions' structure should provide the basis for the four basic elements of missions, namely, mobilizing, training, sending, and partnering.

Structures vary, so it is important to identify the cultural aspects that are involved in your context. Some cultures strongly emphasize egalitarian values and prefer a networking type of structure. Other cultures—and hence the resulting structures—are hierarchical and the thinking pyramidal (i.e., top down). Another structure is the cooperation model, whereby the partners are equal and the roles are clearly divided between them.

For effective implementation, specific people are necessary—e.g., missions' director, missions' committee members, people involved in mission training—and all are key players. The same is true in the field structure.

Not only is the structure important, so is the decision-making process, which affects the brand of the mission. Through defining clear roles and responsibilities, the staff and the clients receive excellent service and are satisfied. The ability to properly delegate and empower others impacts the image of the mission.

Likewise, we need careful consideration in building the financial structure. This includes the support system of the missionaries, financing the education of missionary children, and the support of the mission headquarters. We must give the financial support of the partner careful consideration in order to avoid dependency and the resultant danger of quenching the initiative of the indigenous church.

The best structure will "echo" the glory of God, not human politics or power games. The Church is the bride of Jesus Christ; and its actions must reflect his heartbeat, which John 3:16 expresses, "...that whosoever believes in Him shall not perish but have eternal life." How can they believe if they have not heard the Gospel? We challenge you to develop a missionary sending structure for your country to send missionaries to the ends of the earth!

www.ingramcontent.com/pod-product-compliance
Lightning Source LLC
Chambersburg PA
CBHW060409090426
42734CB00011B/2271